THE 12 STEPS

for
CRYSTAL METH ADDICTS

table of
CONTENTS

4 FOREWORD

8 WHY TWELVE STEPS?

14 GETTING TO WORK

22 THE TWELVE STEPS OF CRYSTAL METH ANONYMOUS

24 STEP ONE
We admitted that we were powerless over crystal meth and our lives had become unmanageable.

36 STEP TWO
Came to believe that a power greater than ourselves could restore us to sanity.

46 STEP THREE
Made a decision to turn our will and our lives over to the care of a God of our understanding.

56 STEP FOUR
Made a searching and fearless moral inventory of ourselves.

74 WHAT ABOUT SEX?
Building a sexual ideal.

82 STEP FIVE

Admitted to God, to ourselves and to another human being the exact nature of our wrongs.

90 STEP SIX

Were entirely ready to have God remove all these defects of character.

98 STEP SEVEN

Humbly asked God to remove our shortcomings.

106 STEP EIGHT

Made a list of all persons we had harmed and became willing to make amends to them all.

114 STEP NINE

Made direct amends to such people wherever possible, except when to do so would injure them or others.

124 STEP TEN

Continued to take personal inventory and when we were wrong promptly admitted it.

132 STEP ELEVEN

Sought through prayer and meditation to improve our conscious contact with a God of our understanding praying only for the knowledge of God's will for us, and the power to carry that out.

140 STEP TWELVE

Having had a spiritual awakening as a result of these steps, we tried to carry this message to crystal meth addicts, and to practice these principles in all of our affairs.

THE TWELVE STEPS

FOREWORD

FOREWORD

Addicts have been following the straightforward suggestions found in the Twelve Steps to recover from all sorts of obsessions—from alcohol and drugs to gambling, overeating, compulsive sex, and codependency—since the 1930s. Crystal meth addicts are no different. The Steps have guided thousands and thousands of us out of misery and into hope.

Bill C. brought a group of us together in Los Angeles in the mid-1990s to start Crystal Meth Anonymous so we could have a home of our own in recovery. Before then, we worked the programs of Alcoholics Anonymous, Narcotics Anonymous, Cocaine Anonymous, and other fellowships. Many of us still attend those programs as well as CMA, and we use their words "sober" and "clean" more or less interchangeably. "A drug is a drug is a drug," we were told: Compulsively using meth is only a symptom of our mental obsession; that's why we abstain from alcohol and all other mind-altering substances as well.

But we didn't always feel free to share in other meetings about parts of our experience that were, well, more colorful. And we often struggled to identify with people whose stories were radically different from ours. Some of us felt too ashamed to even raise our hands. Thanks to those first fellows of CMA, it's possible today to get sober without ever leaving our fellowship. We have meetings around the world and around the clock.

There are many ways a person can get clean or try to lessen the damage drugs are doing in their life—medical interventions, religious approaches, harm-reduction counseling, and other kinds of group support. You'll meet fellows in CMA who've tried them all. But we believe the fellowship and the Steps work best for us. The meetings support us in maintaining abstinence, so our minds and bodies can heal; the program encourages us to take action in our own recovery, so our spirits can heal.

THE TWELVE STEPS

Sponsors lead sponsees through the Steps in CMA, just as they've done since the early days of AA. While our fellowship has amassed a growing collection of stories and other readings that touch on this journey, we haven't written our own guide to the Steps, relying instead on the wonderful literature of the other fellowships. But after three decades, we think it's time we had a guide to the Twelve Steps written by and for crystal meth addicts.

We've been told we must go to any lengths to get sober, but we've also been urged to "go where it's warm," to seek out recovery where we feel like we can relate. When we come to CMA, we hear our own stories. If we didn't identify, we wouldn't stick around. The same is true when we pick up the literature: We connect better when we hear echoes of our common experience.

We also hunger to read about the program in contemporary language that reflects the experience of people in our fellowship, who represent every race, gender, class, sexuality, and ability, and every imaginable belief system. In short, we need a guide to the Steps that describes approaches people in our program use today. It's in that spirit that we offer this book.

To the newcomer: Reading this book, you may encounter language or anecdotes that trigger you. We urge you not to put it away when you run into difficulty—the pages of recovery literature are a safe place to confront our obstacles. We've learned that we cannot avoid triggers forever. If you encounter a passage that troubles you, try to keep it in context; take a deep breath and reach out to your fellows to talk it through if you need to. That's what we did in our early months, and before we knew it, the things that once triggered us didn't trouble us at all.

To the old-timer: Everyone who's worked on this book can attest to something in it—or many things—they do

FOREWORD

not agree with one hundred percent. You may not see your favorite phrase from some other literature; and you will likely wish there was less emphasis on this and more on that. It could not be otherwise. There are as many ways through the Steps as there are people in recovery. We only ask that you keep an open mind.

Whether you're just reading about the Steps for the first time, or you are searching for a fresh perspective on something you thought you knew inside and out, we hope you will see yourself in these pages—and find a solution to the problem we all share.

This book was written and produced by CMA members in New York City with input from fellows around the world and approved for publication by the NYCMA Intergroup. It has not been approved by CMA's General Service Committee and is therefore not Conference-approved literature. This guide is a living document. The writers and editors are already at work on the second edition, which will include an overview of CMA's Twelve Traditions. We welcome your feedback and contributions; please contact *Literature@NYCMA.org*.

THE TWELVE STEPS

WHY TWELVE STEPS?

We had to stop. Crystal meth was killing us. We'd screwed up relationships, lost jobs, sacrificed our health and sanity. Many of us went weeks without sleeping, losing ourselves in the compulsive pursuit of sex. We obsessively picked apart electronics—or picked away at our own skin. Some of us landed in hospitals, jails, or mental institutions, but still we couldn't quit. We blocked the phone numbers of our dealers or using buddies. We vowed that we'd only drink from now on, or smoke weed, or drop molly. We got referrals to see psychiatrists, or cut off people we thought were bad for us, or even moved across country. No matter what we tried, we couldn't escape our problem and put the drugs down.

Some of us were lucky. We arrived at this crisis before things got too awful: We realized that crystal and other drugs were consuming more and more of our time and energy, or watched them devour our friends' lives entirely, and knew clearly what was coming. We could see the terrible truth: On our own, we'd never be able to stop. We needed real help. Someone—a doctor, a friend, a partner—suggested we come to Crystal Meth Anonymous, and we were just hopeless enough to give it a try.

A lot of us weren't sure what to make of the people we met, all smiling and handing us their phone numbers. What did they want? Soon we figured out that they didn't want anything from us, but *for* us: They wanted to help us to get better just as they had. The people in CMA meetings seemed healthy and happy, and generally connected to the world in a way we couldn't even remember feeling. How was that possible?

They weren't that different from us. Some of them, when they shared, seemed to be telling our own stories. Sure, there were differences, but the similarities were overwhelming. They'd been through much of the same misery, known many of the same feelings, reached the same dark places we had. And now, somehow, they were better.

Though it confused us at first, we soon started to pick up their soberspeak, full of concepts like acceptance and surrender and Higher Powers. We began to comprehend the basic tools of recovery, spelled out in all those cute slogans: It seemed sensible to avoid "people, places, and things" that reminded us of using. It made sense to "keep it simple, silly," and not let ourselves get too "hungry, angry, lonely, or tired." We got over ourselves and went out to a diner for fellowship, "the meeting after the meeting." And when the craving to use returned, we found the courage to reach out to our new friends. They told us to "play the movie through to the end," and doing that helped our panic subside.

Trusting others and following their commonsense recommendations, we started getting better, too. Time and again, our fellows offered one suggestion above all. The answer—the one thing that really kept them sober, they said—was printed on those banners hanging in most of our meetings. Were we ready to take a look at the Steps?

GOING TO ANY LENGTHS

We may not have paid much attention to them, only half-listening when the Steps were read aloud. We knew CMA was a Twelve Step program. Why or what that might mean hadn't concerned us. The meetings were helping us; we were getting to know other people who'd been desperate like us, people who'd struggled to get their lives together after catastrophes even worse than our own. Today they were sober, some of them for five, ten, even twenty years or more.

We listened intently as they told us how they'd done it. They had accepted they were addicts, just like we were doing now. They had found a group of other addicts who, miraculously, were staying sober, just as we'd been lucky enough to do. Beginning to trust these people, they finally asked for help. Their fellows had said the Steps were the key, the straightforward instructions to the whole endeavor. Now they were passing the same suggestion on to us.

We didn't realize it, but we'd already begun to do them. If we were staying clean a day at a time by following our fellows' helpful suggestions, we were doing Steps One, Two, and Three in a rudimentary fashion. By now most of us had found a sponsor, and they assured us we were doing great. Now, they told us, it was time to take a good look at those banners and really get to work.

A lot of us charged right in. We'd hit a bottom so gruesome, so dispiriting—and felt such joyous relief now that we weren't using—that we would try anything, do anything to keep from going back. We used to do insane things in pursuit of a high; now we were willing to go to any lengths to get sober. And it felt terrific. Connecting with other people in the meetings, we began to build a network, a sober family. We could rely on them, and more and more, they could rely on us, too. We were feeling like ourselves again; maybe we really could beat this thing!

Some of us landed on what our fellows called a pink cloud. Life wasn't just good, it was *great*. We volunteered for every service position and went to the diner every night with our fellows. We picked up a new self-help book or dove into a new religion every week. We felt so close again to our families and friends, we started dispensing psychological advice. Alas, eventually something happened to dispel our sober ecstasy. Even pink clouds bring rain. Focusing on our Step work helped us weather the ups and downs in our spiritual mood.

Others felt reluctance. We weren't tap-dancing through life, but the days were ticking by, and we felt better and better. The program spelled out in those twelve recommendations seemed like overkill. There was a lot of religious-sounding stuff, as well, that put many of us off. And some of the instructions seemed awfully onerous: Turning our will over?

Doing a thorough inventory? Making amends? We came to CMA to stop doing crystal. Hadn't we accomplished that?

The simple truth is this: We believe we must do the Twelve Steps, or the sobriety we've achieved today will slip away tomorrow. If we're serious about getting better, we will do whatever it takes to prevent a relapse. We've come to believe that using is no longer an option—so we take the suggestion to get to work.

RUNNING-AWAY DISEASE

Addiction is an illness, usually classified as a psychiatric disorder, yet a medical cure remains elusive. Of course, we encourage anyone with a substance-use disorder to seek assistance from doctors and psychotherapists if it's helpful; many of us did and do. But weirdly enough, we achieved more lasting results—true sobriety—only when we let go of the idea that we could be cured. We got better when we became willing to take responsibility for our own treatment.

We think of addiction as a spiritual disease. It often damages our minds and bodies, but it always strikes at our souls. And because its symptoms lead us into various personal and social failures, it's no surprise that people dismiss addiction as some kind of deep character flaw. We suffer from serious stigma all over the world. The miraculous insight of Bill W. and Dr. Bob—the founders of Alcoholics Anonymous, upon which CMA and all other Twelve Step programs are patterned—was to turn this stigma upside down. This spiritual malady, they realized, needed a spiritual solution.

It's fairly straightforward: We have a running-away disease; we use drugs to avoid pain or trauma or just everyday life. But doing drugs becomes a mental obsession that only creates more, and more serious, problems. The farther we run, the more pain and trauma we find. We'll never get better unless we can somehow stop running.

The Steps have taught millions of people how to do just that. Since the 1930s, people have used them not only to find relief from their many specific compulsions, but also to achieve a measure of serenity about life itself that most nonaddicts would envy. It's been said that in active addiction we were already on a spiritual quest: Getting high was our clumsy attempt to find transcendence. But because we couldn't handle life, the instinct to escape soon eclipsed that joyful impulse.

The Steps put our feet back on a spiritual road. They teach us to stop running away from everything, to run toward something instead. What that something might be is up to each of us to discover.

A NEW LIFE

Now that we aren't fleeing from everything, we see that the world around us isn't so terrible. Things that used to be strange and frightening seem exciting and beautiful today. Once, we couldn't focus on anything; now we enjoy our daily routine. Once, we shrank from every challenge; now we have tools to face anything. Once, we were totally isolated; now we're excited to look people in the eye. Once, we gave up on our dreams; now we're open to starting new relationships and new careers. In our noisy lives, we're beginning to hear some lovely harmonies.

When we came in, our fellows told us the program was designed only to help us stop using, so we could bring an end to the rolling disaster our lives had become. It was up to us to take whatever opportunities might follow. If we did, we probably wouldn't recognize ourselves in a few years. Slowly we'd take off the mask we'd been hiding behind and discover our authentic selves. It was a terrifying prospect, but an exciting one, as well.

We took a deep breath and got to work. We hope you will do the same, and like us, find new purpose, freedom, and joy.

THE TWELVE STEPS

GETTING TO WORK

Recovering from our addiction to crystal meth is hard work; we don't deny it. We're willing to do it—to do the Steps—because if we don't, we believe we will use again. And the cost of that is simply too great. But once we get started, most of us find doing the program is a labor of love. Day by day, we begin to glimpse a wonderful new life filled with possibility. Getting and staying clean feels truly miraculous, but we begin to want more than mere abstinence.

If you're like most of us, you probably haven't come to CMA to begin a spiritual quest. You've come to quit using drugs, not levitate to some higher plane. Well, you can relax: Recovery from addiction to crystal meth and other drugs is the only thing we can definitely promise. But what an enormous promise that is! *If we faithfully do the Steps to the best of our ability, we can stay sober.*

So how do the Steps work—or more specifically, how do we work them? Put simply, the Steps bring about an inner change that interrupts the painful cycle of our addiction. When we stop doing drugs, that's only the beginning of our inside evolution. For most of us, working and living the Steps set in motion a profound psychic shift. We can continue to grow and change, becoming entirely new people if we want.

INNER CHANGE

Our story may sound familiar: General discontent led us to fantasies of escape; we picked up drugs, ran away into a binge, and soon crashed; we awoke to remorse and nursed ourselves back to equilibrium; but there we found only the old discontentment. The clock started over, leading us back into the abyss. On it went: Binge, crash, remorse, fantasize, binge, crash…. For some, this journey took weeks or months; for others, it all happened in a day. Some addicts short-circuited the cycle entirely—they became daily users almost immediately, thinking they'd never have to crash—and kept their run going until everything fell apart. Worst of all, even knowing this sorry saga was repeating itself, we were powerless to stop it.

The Steps interrupt this countdown to hell. Step One, truly accepting we're addicts and fully grasping the disaster that awaits when we use, can halt most of us even when we're all alone and at the brink of picking up—but only for a time. We must back away from the brink altogether. In Steps Two and Three, we learn to ask for help. We never need to be alone with our problem. Our fellows, with all their practical suggestions, are just a meeting or a phone call away. They've found a way to stay sober; there's no reason it can't work for us, too. We're much more likely to pick up when we're on our own with our disease. Staying connected to others and a Higher Power of our own understanding keeps us from isolating.

But eventually the day may come when, driven by some emotional upset, we don't reach out. Our resentments grow so large they blot out the inconvenient truth that we're addicts, and our fears cast clouds over the possibility that anyone can help us. We know crystal meth is a false solution offering only more pain, but what if we're too angry or heartbroken to care? The inventory process in Steps Four and Five gives us a way off this roller coaster: We learn how to work out our difficulties with anyone. We never have to get so distraught that we deny reality, shun help, and resort to drugs to run away from our pain.

Steps Six and Seven take us even further away from a relapse: What if we could avoid such upsets in the first place? What if we could reshape instincts that have gotten warped, those self-defeating "character defects" that put us into conflict with others and spark our resentments and fears? This may be the most difficult thing to achieve—we're only human, after all. But even making the attempt to change helps us grow stronger and more serene in the face of difficulties. This is where we begin to find true relief.

The best way to cement our emotional growth so we never feel the urge to run away is to do Steps Eight and Nine. Making amends for the damage and pain we've caused others cleans the slate, spiritually speaking. Maintaining our spiritual condition by diligently working Steps Ten and Eleven, and helping others find recovery in Step Twelve, we can escape the relapse cycle indefinitely.

WORKING WITH A SPONSOR

If it sounds like a lot, don't worry. None of us does this work alone. Thinking we can solve our problems without anyone's interference is a feature of our disease. We call it self-sufficiency or self-will, and it's a great obstacle to our progress. We came to CMA because our way didn't work. We had to ask for help and be willing to take it.

We leaned on many different fellows. But it was key to choose one specific person—a sponsor—to guide us through the Steps. There are no strict rules, but most of our sponsors had been sober for at least a year, meaning they'd been able to get through a range of life situations without picking up. They were simply another recovering addict with a working knowledge of the Steps who was staying sober a day at a time. That was pretty much the whole job description.

How did we choose them? As we got to know fellows at our meetings, we gravitated to people who seemed to make the most sense to us when they shared. Not necessarily the people with the most time, or those who had the most to say. We tried to set aside questions of personality and circumstances: We weren't looking for the most popular person, or the richest, or the sexiest—indeed, sometimes these things proved a distraction. We listened for a person we felt we could click with, someone who "had what we wanted," recovery-wise. A person who was grounded in the program, expressed their gratitude, and seemed able to handle life's challenges as they came along.

Our sponsors usually asked us to call them every day, at least at first. They wanted to get to know us and hear about our journey to the rooms, so they could take us through Step One. They also wanted us to get to know them and get into the habit of reaching out. Learning to trust others and take suggestions would be important in helping us grasp the Steps. Our sponsors each had their own take on the program, colored by their life experiences and the guidance their sponsors had given them. Later, when we became sponsors ourselves, we would bring our own personalities and impressions to the work.

Each relationship is unique. Some days our sponsor feels like a teacher; others, they're a caring older sibling; still others, they're a sober running buddy who might need to lean on *our* shoulder. It's unlike any other friendship we'll ever have. Ours is a "we" program, built on one addict helping another. We reach out to one another and get better together. Few people can understand us the way we understand each other in CMA.

Most of us will have more than one sponsor over the course of our recovery. That's totally fine—it can even be beneficial, allowing us to hear about the program from a variety of perspectives. Our sponsors are not professionals; they give their time to us freely. Their lives may change, or ours. If we do have to switch, we try to find a new sponsor quickly and lean on other fellows in the interim. Some of us put together a "board of directors," a crew we can reach out to when we need clarity about something or guidance making a difficult decision. Whatever our support network looks like, we need to be accountable to others in the program—we can't stay sober on our own.

MAKING THE PROGRAM OURS

In this guide, you will find many suggestions. Doing the Steps at all is simply a suggestion! But we have a very good reason to recommend the program: It's what helps us stay sober. That's the only reason we'll ever urge you to do anything: We did it, and it worked.

Although this is a guide to CMA's Twelve Steps, you will not find rules and regulations in this book. For us, finding the willingness to take suggestions was the key to our progress. In early recovery, we saw that our fellows had been through almost every feeling and crisis we were experiencing; it was natural to ask them how they'd survived and follow in their footsteps. Some of us wanted the program to be like boot camp, with a sponsor who'd tell us to drop and give them twenty. But most of us didn't need to be pushed. Having a strong desire to stop using, we were desperate to get better and began the work eagerly.

Day by day, step by step, we gradually took the program our fellows were giving us and made it our own. Our malady is universal—we are powerless over crystal meth, and using it makes our lives unmanageable—but each of us comes from a unique background and has an individual worldview. So while we're all doing the same program, our path through it is distinctly ours.

But make no mistake, we are doing it. At first, some of us thought we could work the Steps without a sponsor. Or we ignored the suggestion to stay abstinent from all mind-altering drugs, not just speed. Or we skipped the Steps altogether, using the fellowship as a sort of social club. No one could order us to do otherwise. We had to find out for ourselves, sometimes at a very high cost, that we couldn't treat recovery like a part-time job.

In these pages, we offer only a broad consensus about how to approach the Steps. For example, in CMA there is no rule about how quickly or slowly to do them. Some of us were so stuck in self-destructive patterns, our sponsors urged a total immersion in the work, guiding us through in a matter of months. But most of the time, they cautioned us against rushing. The wiring in our brains needed time to heal, and we needed experience putting the principles of each Step into practice.

On the other hand, our fellows warned us about the danger of procrastinating. We wanted to build momentum in recovery; it would be hard to do that if we spent a year on each Step. So even though life got busier and busier the longer we stayed sober, we didn't dawdle in our work. When we finished one Step, we moved on to the next. In short: Each of us, with guidance from our sponsor, finds the pace that's best for us—but we keep it up.

The only requirement for membership in Crystal Meth Anonymous is a desire to stop using. We took great comfort in this in the beginning, knowing that as long as we wanted to give sobriety a try, we had a place in the fellowship. We couldn't see it at first, but by the time we'd been to a few meetings, most of us had already taken a simple but important step: We'd come into the program because we were desperate and *needed* to get better. Starting the Steps, we decided to stay—because we *wanted* to get better.

We had begun a journey using the recovery road map our fellows gave us. It was up to us to decide where and how far we'd go.

GETTING TO WORK

THE TWELVE STEPS

THE TWELVE STEPS

of Crystal Meth Anonymous

The Twelve Steps of Alcoholics Anonymous have been adapted with the permission of Alcoholics Anonymous World Services, Inc. Permission to adapt the Twelve Steps does not mean that Alcoholics Anonymous is affiliated with this program. AA is a program of recovery from alcoholism only—use of AA's Steps or an adapted version of its Steps in connection with programs and activities which are patterned after AA, but which address other problems, or use in any other non-AA context, does not imply otherwise. Find the Twelve Steps of Alcoholics Anonymous at *aa.org/the-twelve-steps*.

THE 12 STEPS OF CMA

1 We admitted that we were powerless over crystal meth and our lives had become unmanageable.

2 Came to believe that a power greater than ourselves could restore us to sanity.

3 Made a decision to turn our will and our lives over to the care of a God *of our understanding.*

4 Made a searching and fearless moral inventory of ourselves.

5 Admitted to God, to ourselves and to another human being the exact nature of our wrongs.

6 Were entirely ready to have God remove all these defects of character.

7 Humbly asked God to remove our shortcomings.

8 Made a list of all persons we had harmed and became willing to make amends to them all.

9 Made direct amends to such people wherever possible, except when to do so would injure them or others.

10 Continued to take personal inventory and when we were wrong promptly admitted it.

11 Sought through prayer and meditation to improve our conscious contact with a God *of our understanding* praying only for the knowledge of God's will for us, and the power to carry that out.

12 Having had a spiritual awakening as a result of these steps, we tried to carry this message to crystal meth addicts, and to practice these principles in all of our affairs.

STEP 1

We admitted that we were powerless over crystal meth and our lives had become unmanageable.

STEP ONE

If you're reading these pages, or you've come to a meeting of Crystal Meth Anonymous, you have likely reached the same impasse we did. Maybe you called it Tina, or ice, or dope—whatever you named it and however you did it, it brought you the same pain, left you feeling the same isolation and helplessness. We got to the point where it seemed life couldn't get worse. Crouching at the bottom of the very deep pit we'd dug for ourselves, and believing we couldn't go any lower, we finally turned our eyes upward. How did we climb out of this mess? We started by admitting we had a problem.

If Step One is a beginning, it also represents an ending. Coming into CMA is usually the last chapter in our using history, the final act in a dark, lonely tale. Each of us meets the story's end in our own time. We might see it in the heartbroken faces of our partners; some of us lose our jobs or homes; physical and mental desperation drive many of us into recovery; others come to our senses in an emergency room—almost dying of an overdose or attempting to take your own life can reveal some stark facts. But many of us experience nothing so dramatic. We just wake up and see how lonely and tired we are, how helpless and hopeless we feel. We catch a glimpse of ourselves in the mirror and wonder, *What happened to me?*

Something has finally shattered our denial, and we're willing to be truly honest about our addiction. Admitting the truth, we take our first, vital step toward recovery.

HITTING BOTTOM

We call this feeling a spiritual bottom. Without reaching one, we would have kept cycling though relapse after relapse, enduring astonishing agonies. More drugs was always the answer; even at the end, we still thought they offered an instant escape from our pain, especially from the suffering we were causing ourselves. Long after using stopped being fun, a lot of us remained chained to our carousel of compulsive sex, mindless tinkering, or neurotic chatter. We went back to crystal again and again, no matter the consequences.

Every now and then, a window would open and we'd see the truth: Nothing was working anymore. Most of us glimpsed this frightening reality many times but turned our back on it. We knew our addiction was progressive; it was only getting worse and worse. And we realized, at least intellectually, that it could one day be fatal. Just the same, even when the truth was staring us in the face, we couldn't stop using.

Until we did. The day finally came when we crawled through that open window and looked for help. No one in CMA could tell us when we were done—it's different for everyone; we try not to compare our journey to anyone else's in a literal way. Maybe we never lost a job or a partner or ended up in jail. Many of us made the mistake of thinking we could keep on using because we didn't look so hopeless on the outside. But it wasn't about our outsides, it was about how hopeless we felt inside. When things were bad enough for us, we asked for help.

Other recovering addicts told us the program wasn't for people who need it, but only those who want it. If we'd walked into a meeting, called the helpline, or picked up the literature, we'd begun to develop the desire to stop using. Where did that desire come from? The people in our life (assuming we had any left) may have been desperate for us to get better. Addicts often try to get clean at the urging of family, friends, or employers; people who care about us usually see we're in trouble long before we do. If we'd been caught dealing drugs or breaking other laws, the courts might have sent us to meetings. But our efforts to recover didn't amount to much until we ourselves wanted to get better. We couldn't truly begin the journey into physical, mental, and spiritual health if we hadn't first taken that other trip, into isolation and despair.

In Step One, we made an honest catalog of our misery. We shined a light on all the reasons we had to quit doing drugs and admitted all of it to ourselves. The point wasn't to wallow in self-pity or glorify our craziness; drug addiction isn't an adventure any sane person wants to take. But we did need to clarify the picture for ourselves. Most of us had endured many dark days when the desire to get clean was sincere and powerful, but brushed off that despair in sunnier times. Step One helped us cultivate a deeper acceptance, a durable desire to stop using.

So, what was the whole story? What happened to us? Most of the time, our sponsors asked us to write it all out. We thought all the way back to the first time we smoked weed or had a beer. We probably started experimenting with drugs in the normal way kids do, looking for fun or trying to fit in. But we were people who desperately needed some solution to help us manage life, to handle pain or mask low self-esteem. So that search for thrills soon became a need to escape and eventually a compulsion. We graduated to other drugs, and they crowded out all the other parts of our life. We were hooked on more—nothing was ever enough.

Once we found meth, we were really in trouble. The drug began to rewire our minds the first time we tried it, unleashing a fearsome psychological craving we couldn't overcome. Soon, even in between runs, thoughts of using filled every waking hour. We reached the point where we lived only to use, and believed we had to use to live.

Our stories vary greatly in the details, but they share two important themes. At a certain point, we became powerless over meth and other substances. Once we used, we had no clear idea when we would stop or what calamities would happen along the way. As a result, our lives were truly unmanageable. You'll hear a lot about powerlessness and unmanageability as you get sober. Recognizing both in your life is key to accepting you're an addict—and starting to recover.

POWERLESSNESS

On a hundred sordid Sunday nights, we swore we would stop. We couldn't miss work again. We couldn't leave the kids to fend for themselves at breakfast. We knew our partner was lying awake worrying about us. We'd thrown away our paraphernalia and deleted our dealer's number, but we still couldn't quit. We had to have one more hit.

This is what we mean by powerlessness: Needing to stop, vowing to stop, and not being able to. If only we could go back to snorting it; or only get high once a month; or give it up and just drink, like a normal person—we tried all these strategies and failed. Our willpower was utterly useless. Crystal meth was much more powerful than we were. We couldn't control it. Just thinking about the drug made our hearts race and our palms sweat.

We thought back over our using pattern. Did getting high occupy our minds even when we were sober? How distracting was it, planning and fantasizing about our next party? Did we bargain with ourselves? Did "I can't start before Friday afternoon" become "What does it matter if I smoke on Thursday night?" If we used crystal as a crutch to juggle several jobs or get through a long shift, did we find ourselves renegotiating when the shift was over? Once we were triggered, a voice in our head assured us that any commitment could be avoided, any promise rationalized away. This is the most insidious thing about our disease: At some point, we were just unable to stop; something mysterious took control of us. Over and over, we'd tell ourselves that this time would be different. Yet over and over, this time was only worse than the time before. And over and over, knowing that more pain awaited, we used again anyway.

It was a sad story, but there was no reason to be ashamed about it. We were people with an allergy to drugs: When the idea occurred to use, we couldn't weigh the pros and cons. The disease amplified thoughts of pleasure and escape and silenced memories of how painful it was the last time we came down and the damage we caused. Our brain, which should have kept us safe, got hijacked.

Our sponsors told us to consider all drugs, not just crystal meth, as we thought back. Ours is a program of complete abstinence for spiritual reasons; we're learning to accept life unmedicated, as it really is. That's why, in CMA, we count our clean time from our last day using any mind-altering substance. But there are practical reasons to treat all drugs the same. Most addicts are risk-takers—we rolled the dice and picked up meth, after all, a drug well-known to ruin people's lives! But that adventurous spirit started long before. It's not that alcohol, marijuana, and poppers are gateway drugs; we're just the sort of people who love running through gates.

Most of us were forced to admit that often, though our central problem was crystal, some cannabis or a beer was the prelude to a run. Our fellows called it the ABCs: "Alcohol becomes crystal." Getting honest about our history with all drugs, some of us decided to attend sister fellowships to look at those parts of our disease. But ultimately our issue was addiction, not any particular chemical. That's why we learned to say "a drug is a drug is a drug." Some people may be able to use other drugs, but we couldn't.

Looking back, though, we saw there was one distinct advantage to being addicted to crystal meth: The problems it brought were undeniable. The highs and lows were truly extreme. A very powerful stimulant, it amped up our system for a long time, until our bodies hit a very hard wall. Whether our runs lasted a couple days or went on for weeks, coming back to reality was brutal. Feeling miserable and facing the chaos of a life put on hold for however long, we swore off using, almost religiously.

Before we found the program, the compulsion to use always came back. It may have taken only a few hours or it might have been many months before we got lost again in another reckless round of chaos and the hopelessness that followed. These slips weren't relapses in the strict sense, not following long periods of clean time; they just felt like more of the same familiar failure and heartbreak. Once we came to the rooms, many of us didn't pick up again—we can and do stay clean!—but almost all of us, in active addiction, knew the experience of wanting to stop but being powerless to do so.

If you've shown up to CMA, chances are good that you know this insanity well. It can, and does, cease. For the great majority of us who work the program, the desire to use does eventually disappear. One day at a time, we learn to take contrary actions when thoughts of drugs arise. We no longer believe the lies our heads are telling us.

Recognizing our powerlessness over drugs is the first key, but we have to work for it. Writing about it isn't easy; denial crops up for all of us. But finally, we admit that, yes, we had tried to stop and been absolutely unable to do so. Strangely, this stark realization feels like a gift. For in our powerlessness we find the first true power of recovery.

UNMANAGEABILITY

Being unable to manage drugs, we soon couldn't manage any other part of life. Incapable of showing up for meals or dates or hospital visits, we alienated our friends and families. We became erratic at work, argumentative and inefficient, and

STEP ONE

soon stopped coming in at all. With all our money going into our next high, we started skipping bills; we were too far gone to care when the landlord slipped an eviction notice under the door. Sometimes, to support our habit, we sold drugs ourselves or stole from others. Eventually, a lot of us landed in jail.

Many of us believed crystal made sex better, but soon it consumed our whole life. Seeking out more and more reckless situations, we perpetually needed antibiotics for sexually transmitted diseases; we got entangled with lovers who hurt us or became violent ourselves; or we overdosed when we mixed in GHB, alcohol, and other party drugs. Many of us abused other drugs in between runs, drinking or taking tranquilizers or smoking pot to even ourselves out, causing all sorts of other problems.

Meanwhile, we forgot the medications we were supposed to take. We didn't eat well and went days without sleep, until our health suffered. The drug ate away at our gums, and a lot of us lost teeth. Those of us who used intravenously got dangerous abscesses and staph infections. The damage to our mental health could be severe: We drifted into psychosis, hiding from hallucinations of helicopters and shadow people or jumping out of windows to escape them. Crashing after a binge stranded us in a hopeless despair. Some of us attempted suicide.

As we cataloged our catastrophes, it was helpful to do a bit of math. How much did we spend on drugs or waste during runs? If we lost jobs, how much income did we miss out on? What were our medical bills like? Did we get arrested? Did we endanger other people? What about our friends, families, and partners—when was the last time we went to a movie or game night with people, or showed up for brunch at Mom's house? Who wasn't speaking to us anymore? We weren't used to thinking of these things as consequences of using. But usually, after we'd accepted that we were truly powerless over drugs, we were able look at our history with a fresh perspective.

A grim truth dawned on us: We thought we used because of all the horrible stuff that happened to us. In fact, horrible stuff kept happening to us because we used. Every story is different. There is no set checklist of unmanageability. Each of us leaves our own unique trail of disasters behind. We're all born with a different tolerance for suffering, but suffer we do, each in our own way.

HONESTY AND ACCEPTANCE

Being honest with ourselves and finally accepting the truth of our situation may be the hardest thing most of us will ever do. On our own, we find it's impossible. That's why we came to Crystal Meth Anonymous.

We don't formally do Step One (or any of the Steps) by ourselves. While the essence of the Step is at work in us the moment we glimpse the truth of our situation, we need help to find the courage to accept it and a bit of guidance to make it stick. There are no rules in CMA, merely a set of sensible suggestions. Some sponsors encourage us to dive into the work after our very first meeting. But usually, they want to get to know us first, let us settle into a rhythm of attending meetings and calling every day, and hearing other addicts share their stories. Generally, by the time we're clean 90 days, most of us have at least started Step One.

And that usually means we start writing. Some addicts record it in a narrative. Others go through a workbook, answering focused questions. The main thing is to put down on paper the central facts of our story. Writing makes it real: What was our relationship, from childhood, with drugs? Did we have much luck trying to control our using? What typically happened when we drank and got high? Where did we end up? It's essential to use vivid details. Addicts have a "built-in forgetter," so we need to make a very specific movie we can play whenever we feel triggered to use. Living in Step One, we have that film ready to roll all the time, so we can answer any craving with a resounding "not today."

At the end of our using, we hit bottom. A window opened into our soul, and we saw exactly how far we'd traveled from ever knowing our true self. Writing out the whole story of our powerlessness and unmanageability, with all the gory details of our degradation or disappointment, opened that window for good, so we couldn't easily shut out the truth again. We needed concrete, working definitions of these ideas, based on our own experience: What did powerlessness and unmanageability mean to us? And how exactly had we gone insane? Not just the paranoia, the hallucinations, the psychosis so many of us experienced. Could we see that our day-to-day choices in active addiction were just bonkers?

Our fellows tell us this is the only Step we have to work perfectly; if the day comes when we forget our powerlessness and unmanageability, we're likely to pick up. But working Step One perfectly only means remembering that we ourselves will never be perfect. Where drugs are concerned, our willpower is useless, and accepting that will take perpetual practice.

We give up any idea that we can ever win a bout with crystal meth. If we get back into the ring with it, the drug will prevail. Staying sober begins with the realization that we can't have any relationship with drugs. We don't reserve a place for them in our fantasy life or future "what ifs," or leave a back door open by maintaining relationships with people we used with. Keeping crystal in our life would be delusional; thinking we have any power over it almost ensures we'll go back to using.

THE TWELVE STEPS

Each day, we make this surrender to reality. We're powerless over drugs, and when we use our lives become unmanageable. So we don't pick up today, no matter what. It's difficult to admit the truth about our situation, but it also brings a tremendous sense of relief. Because it's much harder to keep lying to everyone, especially to ourselves.

We remove the lens of good vs. bad or right vs. wrong, and see things for what they are. We're able to finally grasp the reality of our circumstances, of our life, without getting distracted by the judgments of friends, family, and society. In this way, truth isn't really a thing, etched in stone some-where; it's a process, a mind-set. And in finally learning how to seek and accept this truth, we become prepared to face the additional truths that will come our way as we continue on through all Twelve Steps.

We can stop the nightmare of active addiction. We can stop struggling desperately to keep some fantasy alive in the face of all our pain and loss. We can finally stop running away from the world. So much is waiting for us—health and sanity, self-esteem and self-respect, intimacy and joy. If we can live in honesty, recovery promises us the priceless gift of possibility.

STEP ONE

STEP 2

Came to believe that a power greater than ourselves could restore us to sanity.

Step One helped us see clearly that our approach to living just didn't work. As we fell through the trapdoor of drugs again and again, life got more chaotic and depressing. Crystal Meth Anonymous offered us a way to stop—and stay stopped—a new way to look at the whole world. Our fellows demonstrated that the program worked quite well for those who made a thorough attempt. Not only were they staying sober, they were organized, productive, even happy. Where we were often confused, suspicious, and pessimistic, the new friends we were leaning on seemed clear-sighted, trusting, and hopeful.

We'd been reluctant to trust anything. Nothing we tried seemed to work anymore. Our family and friends had let us down, we thought; some of us, in our psychosis, had even become convinced that everyone was out to get us. But in CMA we found a system of doing things that made sense. Naturally questioning types, we did begin to stress out when people talked about "relying on a Higher Power." What exactly was this power greater than ourselves supposed to be? Our sponsors told us not to worry about it. Focus on just staying clean, they said, and let the program itself be our Higher Power. Our H.P. could be G.O.D.—the Group Of Drug addicts who were helping us stay away from meth a day at a time. Or it might be the Good Orderly Direction we were learning from them. Maybe it was the Gift Of Desperation, which week by week was becoming a Gift Of Dignity.

We have the rest of our lives to talk about theology—if we want to. But that's not really what Step Two is about. The questions we need to ask here are: Do we believe we can be sane again? And do we finally have reason to hope?

INSANITY

As always with the Steps, it's helpful to focus on the language we use. Step Two doesn't promise we will become sane. It says we can be sane again. The program isn't magic; there will be plenty of days when emotions get the better of us. That's OK. The rest of the Steps show us a way out of that chaos.

Our fellows tell us it can take a long time—even a year or more—for our brain chemistry to get back to normal. A lot of us are so spun out, we're even a bit attached to that insanity. We've put down the drug, but can't change our thinking patterns so easily. It can be tough to live in the acceptance of Step One, and stick to the commitment not to pick up, when our moods keep swinging so wildly and our thoughts are racing around the clock. That's why it's so key for us to stick close to the meetings, to lean on our sponsors and other fellows, and to follow their practical suggestions. Slowly, we can break the attachment to the frenzy.

When the writers of the Steps talk about sanity, they mean something deeper than this drug-induced mania and psychosis. Some of us in CMA have a dual diagnosis—in addition to our addiction, we suffer from other mental illnesses. Giving up crystal meth may bring our hallucinations and paranoia to an end, but it won't always cure major depression or a mood disorder. It does make treating our other psychiatric problems a whole lot easier.

But when we were using, all of us went a little bit crazy. So the sanity Step Two is describing is more fundamental—more along the lines of "thinking rationally." Addicts like to say that insanity is "doing the same thing over and over and expecting a different result." Time and again, knowing we'd end up in the same sad mess, we picked up crystal. The madness started before we ever bought a beer, took a hit on the joint that was going around, or called the dealer. "This time will be different," we said, knowing in our heart that this time would be absolutely the same, or possibly worse.

Most of us believe this insanity predated our addiction. The universe equipped each of us to handle life's ups and downs, but at some point, maybe when we were very small children, events intervened and we began to feel out of step. Many of us lived with deep discomfort or even trauma, and eventually we turned to drugs to help us cope or escape altogether. None of our rationales ever made any sense—a meth run never helped any problem. Our bosses were only more irritated when we came back to work (if we still had a job); the trouble at home was only more intense; our loneliness only got deeper. We ran away from difficulties and came back to disasters.

We can arrest our addiction if we find the willingness to work on it, and become an eager, balanced, optimistic person again. Step Two doesn't say that we'll become sane for the first time, but that our sanity can be restored. Knowing this helps us discard our old attitude of victimhood. If we're willing to take action, there is hope: We do not need to stay locked in our insanity. The madness can and will stop.

Guiding us through this Step, our sponsors ask us to think back over our active addiction. In truth, we were insane long before we used; the problem, as our friends in AA say, was "the thinking that preceded the drinking." What were some of our crazy excuses to use drugs? What sorts of things did we do as we struggled to get by and find our next high? We knew what would happen every time we picked up but did it anyway. Life became a complete calamity, yet we were still sure we knew best how to handle our problem. We had to do things our way, marching to our own drum—even if crystal meth was the drummer.

Are we behaving that way now that we've stopped using? Life isn't a walk in the park, but when we compare our clean routine to the way we lived in active addiction, we can see that our choices today are rational and beneficial. What exactly is making life so much easier? It's no big mystery: We've stopped using. And how are we doing that? With the help of the program. We are no longer doing things strictly our way. Day by day, staying clean, we are getting better. A Higher Power, working through the fellowship, is already restoring us to sanity. And it seems possible it can do much, much more.

A POWER GREATER THAN OURSELVES

Now, about that Higher Power. Knowing who or what God is—or if there even is a God—is not actually the point of Step Two. It only says that we "came to believe that a power greater than ourselves could restore us to sanity." Most of us are comfortable accepting that the program itself is such a power. That's all we need to know for now. But we have started having a conversation we probably never imagined we'd have—about spiritual matters. And we're reassured to learn that CMA isn't going to tell us what to think about God.

When we first showed up, we noticed right away that most people in the fellowship were comfortable with the words "God" and "Higher Power," using them almost interchangeably. A lot of us feel real resistance to these terms; we're wary of organized religion and indoctrination of any kind. But even those of us who are religious have a "God problem"—we've been playing God in our own tiny hells.

Our sponsors say the program won't demand anything of us: It doesn't ever require us to have any set definition of our Higher Power. Step Two only sets us on the path to explore our relationship with God or the universe in the remaining Steps. Along the way, we can use whatever language we like, or not talk about it at all if we prefer. Likewise, we shouldn't assume anything about the language our fellows use. Spiritual terms mean different things to each of us. We don't force our ideas on anyone else or scorn people who see the matter differently than we do. Simply put, no one will ever tell us what our H.P. is or is not, or how we're supposed to talk about it. It's just none of their business.

Some of us are still uneasy. People who've been around a while tell us the Twelve Steps aren't a religious program but a spiritual one: A holistic solution to our problems with living. We would do anything in the pursuit of crystal meth—are we willing to at least open our minds to this spiritual perspective if it can help us stay sober?

At any rate, something does help us stay clean in those early weeks. There's the sense that we're finally accepting our situation and reaching for a solution; the comfort of meetings, frank conversations with our fellows, practical suggestions from our sponsor. The collective wisdom of our fellows in CMA (and the other addicts who preceded them in all the other Twelve Step programs) is itself a power greater than we are. Watching it work for our fellows and keep them sober, we begin to have faith that it might work for us, too. And putting this collective wisdom to use—staying connected with other recovering addicts; developing "smart feet," or making it to a meeting no matter what else was going on in our day; identifying our triggers and steering clear—was indeed bringing some sanity back to our lives. What a relief!

The cynics among us find it grating at first when people talk about "sober miracles," but miraculous things are indeed happening. Maybe we've run into an old using friend at a meeting who was even more screwed up than we were, and now they're thriving and happy? With the fog of our own using lifting, we're also taking care of problems that used to bewilder us. We used to require crystal or some other drug to deal with even our slightest mood changes, and now we've gone several weeks or months even without needing it. If that isn't a miracle, what is?

For most of us, this unfamiliar feeling—hope—is just the beginning of our spiritual journey. Our conception of our

Higher Power and how it works in our life will inevitably change the longer we stay sober. We're all working the same Twelve Steps, yet each of us is on our own personal path. Just look around at our fellowship! We are a wildly diverse crew, especially when it comes to spiritual matters, and we all get along fine.

This doesn't mean we don't talk about spirituality. Most of us love to! We're a motley bunch of agnostics, atheists, Christians, Muslims, Jews, Buddhists, and on and on, who are in complete agreement about that Higher Power: We know there are as many conceptions of it as there are people in the fellowship. To bring this point home, our sponsors might ask us to seek out people we relate to and ask them to tell us about their H.P. For some, that power is the God they grew up with. For others it's the majesty of science, the inspiring genius of a pop diva, the spirit of a dead grandparent, the wind whispering in the trees, or the circle of recovering addicts in their home group.

Many of our fellows just call it love. For as different as their conceptions are, they often use that word to describe it. They say their Higher Power is kind, compassionate, forgiving, reliable. In our meditations, we ask what qualities our H.P. might have.

By this time, the only thing we know for certain is that whatever God is, it definitely isn't us. And when we are on our own and need a bit of courage or comfort, we take our sponsor's suggestion to just breathe. Our life is in our breath—our "spirit," in Latin. Is there any concept more powerful than that? The easiest way to get in touch with the universe is to simply pause, say thank you, and take a deep breath.

FAITH AND HOPE

As our lives improve in CMA, our hope becomes a vivid belief that life can get better. We trust that the program, which has worked so beautifully for so many people over the decades,

STEP TWO

will work for us, too, if we give it our all. That belief in the fellowship soon broadens into a faith in the ideas or energy we believe are at work within it. We can't always get to a meeting; our sponsor doesn't always pick up the phone. Sometimes our faith is all we have to see us through a challenge.

So when our sponsors tell us not to stress out about finding a Higher Power, they mean it. Only keep an open mind, they say. Our growing faith in the program and the time we spend pursuing the Good Orderly Direction of the Steps will naturally lead us to deeper reflection on the question. In Step Two, we're told we will come to believe in "a power greater than ourselves." As we've said, the language in the Step is very deliberate: It's not *the* power but *a* power—something we find we can rely on, the "God of *our* understanding" described in the rest of the Steps. Our relationship with it isn't fixed; it will change as we change.

Religious people, asking for concrete help from the God of their understanding, feel their convictions deepen. Sometimes God has been only a beautiful abstraction, even for the devout. But the addict sees tangible proof in recovery that their prayers do get answered—though not always as they imagine they will be!—and God is no longer a remote figure in a holy book. Agnostic people, on the other hand, often become more passionately so. They go deeper into the mystery of the universe: Not knowing for them is the whole beautiful point; any god they could thoroughly comprehend just wouldn't be powerful enough. Atheists find their own sublime spirituality, drawing power from their ancestors and heroes, or from astral mechanics, or the changing of the seasons, or the mighty rhythm of the pounding surf.

Our conceptions can change radically. Most of our God problems were caused by other people; now that we're developing our own relationship with spirituality, we can consider the question from our individual perspective.

A committed atheist might find herself joining an orthodox synagogue. A Catholic priest may discard his collar and become a Jungian analyst. As long as our faith in recovery is growing, it's all good. Some mystery keeps us in sync with the rest of our Group Of Drug addicts. If we are connected again to life and not running away from it, something is working. If we find ourselves more and more sane with each passing day, that's all we need to know.

KEEPING AN OPEN MIND

If this all sounds like a lot, don't worry. We will not answer the riddle of the universe today, or ever. So we keep it simple for now: Do we see people in CMA getting better? Their recovery may seem baffling still, but do they have something—peace of mind, discipline, joy—that we want? And how are we doing? Are we better able to shrug off thoughts of using? Does life seem more manageable now that we're sober? When we do feel unbalanced, are we able to offer ourselves some forgiveness and acceptance? Are we more hopeful, and more sane, today?

The answer to all of these questions is probably yes. And with each yes, we find a bit more faith. In Step Three, we'll learn how to turn that faith into a practical, everyday tool.

STEP TWO

STEP

Made a decision to turn our will and our lives over to the care of a God of our understanding.

In Step One, we got honest about what had happened to us and admitted defeat. In Step Two, we recognized a better way of living and started to believe it could make us sane. Step Three offers us a big challenge: Are we willing to give this new approach a try?

Maybe you're thinking, *Wait a minute. Steps One and Two were hard work—I'm already trying!* Indeed you are. If you've started working the program, then you're already doing Step Three. You've been willing to get rigorously honest about all the ways your approach to life hasn't worked and opened your mind to consider that the way people do things in CMA does seem to work. It sounds like you are pretty willing indeed.

But it's not that easy. Nobody comes skipping happily into their first Twelve Step meeting. Walking through that door was the hardest thing many of us had ever done. Even so, that was just admitting we were sick. Step Three asks us to accept the suggestion to take action to get better. Are we ready to surrender? To give ourselves over to the program and everything else our Higher Power is showing us? If we've been running our own affairs for however many years—in other words, if we are human—this may seem like a Herculean task.

MAKING A DECISION

Given the magnitude of the job, the authors of the Twelve Steps offered us a brilliant and beautifully honest caveat. They didn't write, "Turned our will and our lives over…." No. Just, "*Made a decision* to turn our will and our lives over…." No one who's ever lived has always been in total concert with the rhythm of the universe. Being human means having contrary instincts and sometimes acting upon them. So we start this Step understanding that we're never going to be devoid of self-will, the imperious urge to get what we want, to always have things go our way. (You can call it egomania, if you prefer the psychiatrist's term.) We'll never be a robot, and we'll never be an angel. In recovery, we strive for "progress, not perfection."

We recognize that letting our self-centered impulses rule our lives resulted in catastrophe. But some of us still rebel a bit at this point. Are we joining some kind of cult? If we really surrender ourselves this way, what will become of our individuality, our creative spark? We're quite fond of all our lovely rough edges! Well, when we look around the rooms, we find plenty of fiercely independent people—and quite a few glorious eccentrics. "To thine own self be true," Shakespeare says. Quite right: Getting clean, we are putting ourselves in the care of our Higher Power; but our H.P. is taking good care that we learn how to care for ourselves.

The truth is, if we don't try to get sober, we might never put away our masks and draw closer to our real nature. So, with a growing faith that the program can work for us, we decide to at least try to "turn things over." And the moment we make that decision, something miraculous happens. By now, following sober suggestions is working. We decide not to pick up one day at a time; taking directions from our fellows, we find we can do it. We decide to change our phone number so our dealers and using buddies can't reach us. We decide to go eat after the meeting, so we can start making new, sober friends. We decide to take a commitment as a greeter at our home group, so we'll have something regular to show up for.

In the interest of cutting back on drama that might trigger us to use, our sponsors challenge us to turn other things over, too. We don't have to respond to that idiotic email from our boss. We don't need to take the bait when Dad brings up politics. We can let our cousin make the potato salad if it means so damn much to her. We learn to be more methodical about small decisions and big ones. Taking a more rational approach to things, we find life is getting calmer, our difficulties easier to handle. We are beginning to trust ourselves again.

Where we once feared everything, now we're beginning to have a little faith and a lot of hope. We can get better. We can stay sober.

SERENITY

The sensible suggestions our fellows give us have indeed helped us avoid drama. But what do we do when drama won't avoid us? Our ex shows up with no warning. The landlord raises the rent. We run into our old dealer. Things happen. At moments like this, we need help. Sometimes, we need to find the willingness to do a truly difficult thing we'd rather avoid. We don't always trust ourselves to make the right choice, especially when we're first getting sober. Other times, we've got to do nothing—to stop ourselves from reacting when our usual impulses are likely to get us into trouble. We've run away from pain and confusion our whole lives—learning to sit in some emotional discomfort is one of the biggest challenges we face in early recovery.

In such situations, we've learned to pray. As we discussed in Step Two, who or what we pray to is our business—the point is to reach out to whatever Higher Power we trust and ask for help. Since the 1930s, people in recovery have relied on one brief, simple prayer of acceptance and surrender. If you've been coming to meetings for even a short time, you already know it:

God, grant me the serenity to accept the things I cannot change, courage to change the things I can, and wisdom to know the difference.

Saying the Serenity Prayer to ourselves can be incredibly calming when our blood pressure jumps. Our sponsors encourage us to take this prayer out of the meetings and use it in our daily lives. The prayer prepares us psychologically to accept whatever situation we find ourselves in. To make the best choice we can and then let go of the results. To deal with life on life's terms. There may be no better tool for a spun-out newcomer than to consciously pause our thoughts to say these calming words. Our racing minds need the reprieve!

Maybe, our fellows suggest, we can start the morning with it, right when we get out of bed? Using it as a meditation to set our intention every day, we slowly begin to change. We notice we're calmer. Soon, the words spring to mind anytime we encounter some difficulty. Where once we overreacted to every upset, now we take a deep breath…and do nothing. Or we take a deep breath…and do the next right thing, following through with the task at hand.

That's how it goes on a good day—but many times, being human, we will still be prone to spit out the thing we shouldn't say, or make a scene, or drive off in a huff. We may continue to have a hard time taking direction or admitting we're wrong about something—addicts are not famous for accepting authority figures. It's OK. Every day gives us an opportunity to open our minds a little wider. Every day brings new chances to try again.

BEING TEACHABLE

In the last line of the Serenity Prayer, we ask for the "wisdom to know the difference" between things we must accept and things we should change. Wisdom is not at all the same thing as smarts. We only gain it with time, with experience. In the prayer we ask not only for serenity and courage, but also for more teachable moments of failure or success, so that in the future we'll intuitively know what to do in any situation. We hope to do the right thing, and failing that, we hope to learn from our mistakes.

STEP THREE

There are countless wonderful prayers touching on this idea that we grow only through acceptance and surrender. For decades, people in Alcoholics Anonymous have used the following:

God, I offer myself to You—to build with me and to do with me as You will. Relieve me of the bondage of self, that I may better do Your will. Take away my difficulties, that victory over them may bear witness to those I would help of Your power, Your love, and Your way of life. May I do Your will always.

This might be a bit religious-sounding and grand for some tweakers, but the imagery is powerful. Recovery offers us an escape from the prison of self-obsession. And what could be more marvelous than thinking of even our most personal victories as an opportunity to help others?

Others prefer this much simpler formulation, from Narcotics Anonymous:

Take my will and my life, guide me in my recovery, show me how to live.

Acceptance doesn't need to be some fatalistic exercise—we can be eager about it. Here's the plainspoken Mychal's Prayer, which suggests a life of constant growth and perpetual education:

Lord, take me where You want me to go; let me meet who You want me to meet; tell me what You want me to say; and keep me out of Your way.

There are countless wonderful prayers; in CMA we use the ones that work best for us. And if we can't find a prayer that works for us, we can always write our own, tailoring the words to our own background, worldview, and hopes. Here are some of our fellows' prayers:

Higher Power, let me be teachable.

God, please protect me from me.

Today let me follow the rhythm of the universe. Let me give more than I take. Let me teach and be taught. Let me love and be loved.

Of course, many of us don't even call what we're doing prayer—we are setting an intention, grounding our consciousness, or just taking a moment. In our millions of different ways, we're nurturing a spiritual perspective that will help us with our day-to-day challenges, because periodically we need a reminder: On this trip, we aren't in the driver's seat.

LETTING GO

We all want to get our way. And that's great: There's nothing wrong with being ambitious or competitive or seeking affirmation. But given that everyone else on Earth also wants their way, all of us are going to experience many, many disappointments, usually by the time we leave kindergarten.

To help us get a longer view on this issue of willpower, our sponsors may ask us about times we went after something but didn't get what we wanted. It's useful to describe these situations and then tell what happened instead. Maybe we're still angry about not making the basketball team. But that meant we tried out for the school play, and we started exploring the arts. Or maybe we still feel pangs of heartbreak thinking about someone who dumped us years ago;

but if they hadn't, we never would have met the person we ultimately married. Maybe the candidate we wanted lost badly in the last election, but talking over our disappointment inspired us to become an activist and brought a whole new network of interesting people into our life.

We get wedded to outcomes—some of us call this future-tripping—but if those outcomes don't arrive, we needn't be devastated. Practicing Step Three, we begin to have faith that we can survive any eventuality. We surrender to each new lesson and put it to use. Doing Step One, we admitted we were powerless over drugs and alcohol—but the truth is, we're powerless over everything but our own choices. We can't control what other people will say and do, any more than we can control the tides or juggle the moon and stars. All our lives, we've clung to a power we just don't have. Can we learn to let it go?

Slowly, our perspective is shifting. More and more, we're able to accept situations that once would have made us crazy. Acceptance isn't automatic, by any means; we need to consciously change our attitude. One great way to stop focusing on what we don't have and what's not going our way is to write a short gratitude list. Some of us do it every morning. Turning our gaze toward three or four things we're grateful for—anything from waking up sober to having a roof over our heads to going on a hot date or enjoying an everything bagel with cream cheese—puts us in a better frame of mind to deal with difficulties big and small.

HONESTY, OPEN-MINDEDNESS & WILLINGNESS

The most important decision we make at this point is to stay clean and keep working our way through the Steps. There is no more tangible evidence that we're willing to surrender to our Higher Power. Many of us in recovery call Step Three the key to the whole program. This is where we really make a commitment to go to any lengths to get better. We may have had what our fellows call reservations—fears that recovery couldn't work for us, or wouldn't be worth hanging onto if life suddenly took a hard turn—but now we find we can set them aside. We are ready to dive into the next phase of our development, the inventory process of Steps Four and Five. From here on out, our willingness will only grow.

By now we have the H.O.W. of recovery: Honesty, Open-mindedness, and Willingness. We've learned we must be rigorously honest about our disease and become more comfortable sharing about our challenges with our fellows. We've opened our minds to a solution that seems to work, seeing for ourselves the wisdom in suggestions from our sponsor and other fellows. Finally, we're willing to give the whole thing a go, to surrender our pride and follow the program's instructions. We're ready to dive into action.

STEP THREE

STEP

4

Made a searching and fearless moral inventory of ourselves.

STEP FOUR

Practicing Step One daily—honestly accepting that we are helpless in the face of crystal—puts a solid barrier between us and drugs. But admitting the problem isn't enough on its own. Falling prey to self-sufficiency or isolation, we may eventually deny the truth and use again. That's where Steps Two and Three come in. They give us a new spiritual focus, a plan, and a network of like-minded people we can count on. We're no longer alone with our problem. Staying honest, open-minded, and willing, we can survive the intense cravings that strike in early recovery.

But so far, we're addressing only the most pronounced aspects of our disease, our insane compulsion to use and the proud self-reliance that keeps us from getting the help we need. Sooner or later, an emotional upset will come along that could undermine our defenses: We're fired from a job, our partner leaves us, or some other calamity happens, and we feel powerless. Our old solution, to run away into a binge, may suddenly loom large.

Our problem, ultimately, is that we are human. We need a certain amount of material and emotional security to thrive. When our instincts for shelter, comfort, or intimacy feel threatened we can panic. Our fight-or-flight response kicks in, and suddenly life feels like a wildlife documentary, with a leopard chasing us down. It's just the way we're wired: The same instincts that helped us survive in the jungle continue to operate in our civilized brains. And as addicts, who throw alcohol and drugs at every feeling, we've tied those circuits into knots. We've got to uncross those wires and learn to handle distressing situations, or we probably won't stay sober.

That's why we promptly get to work on the next Steps. Steps One, Two, and Three usually have a profound effect on our psyche, but they're largely reflective. Now it's time to move into action. And that will require a lot of

THE TWELVE STEPS

courage. In Step Four, following our sponsor's instructions, we will examine our past, writing about all of our resentments, defects, and fears, as well as our assets. We'll share what we learn with them and our Higher Power in Step Five.

We often think of these Steps as a pair; few of us are able to sit in silence and write everything out without needing some help organizing our thoughts. Understanding our part in our resentments and giving names to our character defenses and fears is challenging. When we aren't able to see the truth, our sponsors can help take the blinders off. They will always meet us "where we are at," but following their directions—being willing to take guidance—is itself an important tool for our spiritual growth. All of which is to say, we don't do this alone.

MORAL INVENTORY

The hardest part for a lot of us to swallow about the inventory is that troublesome word "moral." Haven't our fellows been telling us addiction is a disease and not a moral failing? It's true. We have a mental obsession that leads to all sorts of problems—exhaustion, malnutrition, infections, depression, and psychosis, most of which can be treated with good medical care. But what about the symptoms of the obsession itself? Consider our behavior in active addiction: the lying, stealing, cheating, and betraying, the general disregard for ourselves and others. People aren't exactly wrong to call these "moral" lapses.

But we don't need to trip over others' standards. We aren't confessing sins; we're taking stock, like a shop owner. We know in our heart the way things really were, "the right and wrong" of our actions. What we're making is a truth inventory.

The people who developed the Steps had a remarkable insight: Addiction is that rare illness that can be arrested if we treat the symptoms, in this case, our warped behaviors.

STEP FOUR

We begin to do this by examining our impulses and fears, the stuff we used over. When we've tried to get sober before, we were often driven by shame or remorse about the things we'd done. It didn't work; guilt by itself is truly a wasted emotion. What if we could unlearn the behaviors that caused the remorse in the first place? If we can learn to deal with conflicts and right-size our grandiosity and fears, we never need to fall to pieces again—or use as a result.

The healing begins with "a searching and fearless" examination of our past. It's a daunting job, but we don't put it off. Even if no disaster strikes, having no day-to-day outlet for our family difficulties, work frustrations, or romantic disappointments can be poisonous. Some of us may have been sober for many months by now, but we're still prone to wallow in our troubles instead of taking the next right action. An old-timer who helped get CMA started in New York used to say to us in her exquisite Brooklyn accent, "Honey, you're pregnant with your Fourth Step." It's a shame to go through life stewing over every little conflict, but it would be a tragedy to pick up over them.

PEN TO PAPER

There is power in putting an actual pen to paper when we write out our inventory. Some of our sponsors even insist on it: Handwriting slows our thinking down, and that can be beneficial for the sped-up brain of a meth addict.

There are lots of approaches to doing the inventory, and lots of helpful workbooks and other guides, but however our sponsors guide us through it, we'll need to write things down. Here we will outline the traditional approach a lot of us use in CMA, the famous table with five columns devised by AA's founders. (There's a sample inventory along these lines on page 66.) A lot of sponsors had us go through the inventory column by column; this helps us recognize the patterns we've repeated in our lives. Others prefer working row by row, so we wrap up each resentment as we go along. We can go over our work with our sponsor whenever we have questions; many of us do it when we reach the end of each column or get through several rows of similar resentments.

It's time to start writing. But first our sponsors remind us of a key thing: This is a compassionate enterprise, one of the kindest things we can do for ourselves. We aren't making a list of all of our terrible parts, only describing objectively the things we did when we were out of balance. We're writing down the facts of our past exactly as they happened. No need to retraumatize ourselves dredging up old feelings; there might be time to do that with a therapist. This is just a list, and we should treat it as a list. When the work is challenging, we remember what our fellows have said: Like everything else in the Steps, this is a way for us to find freedom.

COLUMN 1: WHO?

We start by putting down the names of everyone we believe has hurt us. For some, the list is short, maybe a dozen people. For others, it can run to 100 names. It isn't, as a wise sponsor once said, "a list of everyone we've ever met." We try to include only people we truly resent.

The etymology is helpful: To resent means "to feel again." We may have had all sorts of conflicts in the distant past; if an unpleasant feeling about someone has long since faded, we may not need to hash it out again. But if it seems we're whitewashing the past, our sponsors will encourage us to take another look at some of those ancient wounds. When in doubt, we use the elevator test: We imagine the doors opening in front of us and the person in question stepping off. If seeing them would give us a nasty surprise and we just wouldn't know what to say, they belong on our list. For most of us, there are people who arouse feelings we have difficulty

STEP FOUR

describing. We put them down, too. Our sponsors can help us figure it out as we go along.

If we're going column by column, it's useful to organize the people from our past into categories: Family members, friends, colleagues, spouses, sex partners, using contacts, and so on. If we can't remember someone clearly (crystal meth addicts often have gaps in our memory!) we put them down anyway. Some of us also list institutions—churches, schools, agencies, or political parties—or even forces, ideologies, and other abstractions. Racism, misogyny, transphobia, and other bigotries might show up on our list, or sickness and death, or God. It's easy to blame a faceless villain, to feel powerless and sit in toxic feelings, or worse, to play the victim. All the more reason to write these resentments down. If anyone or anything has hurt us, it belongs on our list.

Most of us, at the bottom of our list, put our own name. In active addiction, we were our own worst enemy. But long before we picked up crystal, we harbored deep hostility to ourselves. We are only human; treating ourselves kindly will be a lifelong job.

COLUMN 2: WHAT?

In the second column, we describe exactly how each of these people or entities hurt us. This is one spot in the Step work that may feel a bit like therapy. We let it all out—all the ways our parents were terrible, how our friends let us down, how our bosses mistreated us, how our partners cheated.

We may relish the chance to lay out all our grudges, but we try not to dwell on it. In the first place, this part of the inventory can be painful. Some of the memories still sting; we need to move through our discomfort to find the relief on the other side. When we start to linger in bad memories, our sponsors remind us that setting aside our victimhood is the goal. We spent enough time in active addiction mulling over past wrongs. Most of us find we can't just snap our fingers and forget about the horrible experiences we've lived through. But trauma and resentment, as we'll soon see, are very different things. Here, we are acknowledging our pain, not giving in to it. We don't need to write an endless essay, in other words. Simple bullet points are enough.

By our own name we may make a lot of notes. How have we let ourselves down? Not just in our addiction—by now, we're done beating ourselves up for picking up crystal. What other bad choices have we made? Have we disappointed others and ourselves, fallen short of our goals, abandoned our dreams? Do we cling to internalized bigotries? What false stories have the voices in our heads been telling us?

COLUMN 3: WHERE?

Where did we feel the hurt? Which instinct was wounded? Our fundamental self-esteem or our pride? Our need for security, our financial or professional ambitions? Our personal or sex lives? It's illuminating to think of our conflicts in these terms: how our needs and desires have been blocked. We consider the instincts that felt threatened and write them down.

People have hurt us, no doubt, but considering our resentments from this perspective may help to de-personalize them, reminding us of our basic humanity. It also helps us understand the people we resent. Seeing how we've gone through life obeying human instincts, we begin to recognize that they've been doing the same thing. Just like us, our parents, lovers, and employers came by their reactions honestly. Understanding that, and recognizing our common humanity, may help us begin to forgive them.

COLUMN 4: MY PART

Now that we've spelled out our injuries, our sponsors have news we may not want to hear. No doubt, people have mistreated us

STEP FOUR

and hurt us, sometimes deeply. But there isn't much we can do about it. We don't have a time machine; even if we did, we'd be very unlikely to change the people in our lives. Some of them have no idea they've hurt us anyway. A lot of us ask ourselves, what exactly is the point of this trip into history? We can't alter any of it!

Well, it is true that we can't undo the past. But we can rewrite our relationship with it. There is one thing we always have the power to change: what we do. We've always been comfortable blaming others, but how has that served us? Every conflict has two sides—are we willing to look at our part? We must be if we want to grow emotionally and spiritually. If we can't approach our resentments from a new perspective, we'll be doomed to the self-pity and anger that so often fueled our using.

Sometimes the role we played is obvious. In almost every instance, we helped get the ball rolling in one way or another. When the things that happened "on our side of the street" aren't clear, we ask the following questions: Where have we been selfish or self-seeking? When were we dishonest or inconsiderate? What fears drove our reactions?

There are many situations where the other party didn't really do anything at all. Our resentment is attached to something we're ashamed of—something we thought, something we did that they may not even know about. Or it could be that we envy them for some reason—they did better at school, they got the promotion we wanted, they married our ex. We've manufactured crimes for them to justify our disregard when our real obstacle is our own expectations or sense of entitlement.

On the other end of the spectrum, there are cases where we did nothing at all. We aren't responsible for someone else's violence, abuse, mental illness, or prejudice. But we do have a role to play in our own healing, no matter how intense the

65

trauma was. Is there some action we might have taken action to help ourselves get better?

Though we might not have had a part in the incident, we always have a part in the resentment about it. When it comes to events that are far in the past or otherwise abstract, continuing to nurse the grudge is entirely on us. We can't forgive our parents, for example, for divorcing when we were small, so we ignore their phone calls or put off visits. The popular girls in junior high gave us a homophobic nickname, and decades later we remain dismissive of a lot of women we meet. We relish gossiping about the guy our ex-wife married. We're constantly telling people how awful that restaurant is that fired us for using at work.

Once we set our part down against the other person's, it becomes clear that we aren't blameless in most of our relationships, and it's time to stop playing the victim. In some cases, though we feel no rancor toward people, we're suffused with regret nonetheless. We're ready, even eager, to reach out to old friends we've grown apart from. We feel forgiveness stirring in our hearts, even toward people we thought we never wanted to see again. Our sponsors assure us there will be time to make amends and heal broken relationships later in the Steps.

COLUMN 5: CHARACTER DEFECTS

In the last column, we consider each resentment and *name* our behaviors, describing the specific ways we lashed out at others and injured ourselves. We call these character defects or shortcomings, but a lot of us find it more useful to think of them as defense mechanisms or negative reactions. How do we behave when we feel cornered?

Many people start with the seven deadly "sins" from literature—pride, anger, greed, gluttony, lust, envy, and sloth—but there are lots of other adjectives we can use. Were we self-centered, judgmental, vindictive, gossipy? Careless, passive-aggressive, aloof? Were we sometimes racist, sexist, homophobic, transphobic? We use the words that resonate for us, and when we're confused about how to name a behavior, we ask our sponsor for help. What we are compiling is a tidy list of all the defenses we've habitually resorted to. This is actually the whole point of the inventory: Finding a better way to operate today and in the future starts with understanding the flawed way we operated in the past.

This last column is also a good place to ask ourselves: What is or was behind our behavior? Some warped instinct triggered these defense mechanisms. What exactly were we so afraid of? Many of us jot that down, too: fear of intimacy, fear of abandonment, fear of failure, fear of success. As we'll see soon, identifying these fears is one of the most useful parts of the whole process.

OUR SIDE OF THE STREET

The Fourth Step inventory gives us a lot of information. We've noted all the ways we've been hurt and considered which instincts felt most threatened. But rather than dwelling on the old idea that others caused all our problems, we focused on the things we did to contribute to conflicts and how we cultivated recriminations after the fact.

After all this digging through the past, a lot of us are understandably eager to put down the shovel. Our introspection and analysis have left us in a place we've avoided, consciously or unconsciously, for our whole lives: our own side of the street. It feels strange, uncomfortable, maybe even a bit scary to look at the world from over here. *(Continues on page 68)*

THE TWELVE STEPS

A SAMPLE INVENTORY USING
THE FIVE-COLUMN TABLE

WHO *Who hurt me?*	WHAT *What did they do to me?*	WHERE *What instinct was blocked?*
Mom	Emotionally distant then; very needy now; liked my brother better; made me get a job	Ambition, Security, Intimacy, Self-esteem
Chris, *my ex*	Cheated on me; ran me down to our friends; drug addict	Security, Sex life, Self-esteem
Kate, *my boss*	Suspended me for being late; didn't give me a raise; not as smart as I am	Security, Ambition, Finances
The Police **& the DA**	Arrested me for dealing. If I lose my court case, I could go to prison!	Ambition, Security, Self-esteem
Rick, *college* *friend*	All through college, he'd use a racial slur around me, like he was joking about being racist—it was just racist	Self-esteem, Security, Intimacy
Jane, *a friend*	Bailed on me on my birthday; looks down on me for using	Intimacy
The **church**	Told me I was going to hell!	Security, Sex life
Me	Couldn't stop using; blew so many interviews; I quit everything I do; cheated on Chris; got so sick the last time I binged I ended up in the ER	Intimacy, Ambition, Security, Sex life, Finances

STEP FOUR

MY PART *What role did I play then? How do I nurse this grudge?*	CHARACTER DEFECTS *How did I act out? What was I afraid of?*
I knew things were hard after Dad left, but wasn't any help anyway. She didn't actually like my brother better—he was just easier to deal with. Now I don't return her calls.	Selfish, angry, jealous, judgmental, procrastinating Fear that I'm like her
I retaliated and cheated on him. Told his parents he'd been fired. It was my idea to try meth in the first place. I make fun of his new boyfriend. Blame my dating problems on him!	Angry, lustful, selfish, dishonest, gossipy Fear of intimacy
I am always late—even sometimes now that I'm sober! I look for evidence she's an idiot instead of focusing on the things she does well.	Procrastinating, disrespectful, angry, careless, judgmental Fear of poverty
Um…I was dealing. I knew the laws and broke them anyway. Dealing meth is a dangerous, careless thing.	Careless, self-seeking, reckless Fear that I'm a screwup
I never told him to stop. I just laughed along like I didn't care. When I ran into him last year he seemed more evolved, but I purposely tried to make him feel stupid.	Avoidant, selfish, timid Fear of confrontation
How many times did I rush to her to rescue me after a binge? And how many dates with her did I blow off?	Selfish, thoughtless Fear of being judged
I assume religious people are bigots when I know plenty who aren't. I'm so angry about dogma, I won't admit the church taught me some good lessons, too.	Judgmental, aloof, angry Fear of being an outcast
<<<< See column two. I guess I have a knack for self-sabotage! My denial about my drug problem was pretty deep.	Procrastination, denial, self-centeredness Fear of success and of failure; fear of intimacy, being alone

We take a deep breath. There's still much more to learn. Now, our sponsors tell us, it's time to look at our inventory from some different angles: We need to explore the fears that lie underneath all our resentments. We need to also look at the total opposite side of the ledger and consider our assets.

FEARS

In itself, fear is no crime. In fact, it's one of the most important human instincts, alerting us to danger and pointing us to safety. In the First Step we even cultivated one very healthy fear—the fear of relapse. But not all fears are beneficial. Sometimes the danger they're alerting us to isn't really there, and the safety they send us toward isn't safe at all. False fears keep many meth addicts from seeking recovery and, later, lead countless others to relapse. In active addiction our lives were so steeped in danger that we lived comfortably with all sorts of terrors. We couldn't see that they were driving us further and further into risky territory: hopelessness, self-pity, shame, and denial.

Our sponsors warn us that we can't unlearn this instinctive anxiety overnight. But they do have some good news: When we take an inventory of just our fears—of death or illness, of deprivation, of failure or success, of abandonment or suffocation—some heartening truths will emerge. Horrible stuff has likely come to pass for all of us: Our parents have seriously let us down, or we've failed miserably at jobs, or had to beg relatives for money to pay back debts, or been kicked out of the house by our partners, or much, much worse. But we survived, despite the deep conviction we would not. Most of our fears, it turns out, are overblown. They're lies we've told ourselves to explain our flawed understanding of life.

Some sponsors talk us through our fear inventory, but many tell us to write out a finite list of the exact fears that drive our character defects. The list may begin with any fears

STEP FOUR

we put down in the moral inventory, but we probably need to go further. Thinking about the main areas of our life, finances and career, romances and friendships, family and self, we ask some questions. Are we afraid of being poor or overlooked, or having too much responsibility and success? Are we frightened of intimacy—or being alone? When it comes to ourselves, are we afraid of being demeaned by others? Or having people find out about some not-so-great thing we did?

Once we've got a list, we ask: What triggers each fear? What situations bring it into our minds? As we did in the resentment inventory, we ask what part of our life feels threatened: Our security or finances? Our personal and sexual relationships? Our pride and self-esteem? What happens when we have this fear—how do we react? Take the fear of failure: Do we puff ourselves up, become angry, fall into self-pity? Do we isolate, or create lies to make ourselves look good? Every fear drives reactions, and most of them are not useful. They don't dispel the anxiety or address the underlying concern.

Next we ask: What is the belief driving the fear? What story have we told ourselves—that we now believe wholeheartedly—that brings this fear out the moment we get a hint of confirmation? Say we have a fear of failure that flares to life after our boss offers us some constructive criticism: She just wants us to get a little training, but all we can hear is that we aren't good enough, we're a fraud, good things won't ever happen for us.... When we uncover beliefs like these, we can see they really aren't true. With our sponsor's loving guidance, we can set aside these false stories and pick up new ideas based in reality.

Some of us write prayers or affirmations to reach for when our old fears return, because they will return. This is a lifelong job. Our fears are powerful and persistent, but the spiritual principles we're learning as we continue in the

Steps are even stronger. In time, our fears will begin to fall away and no longer rule us as they once did. We find the courage to face them. Soon we even have faith. Faith that the dark experiences of our past can become useful to us in the present. Faith that all the resources we'll need in the future are waiting for us. Faith that we can meet any fear without running away.

ASSETS

Seeing clearly that most of our fears are false opens up a new perspective. It turns out there are many things we did (and do) well. As we've said, the original authors of the Twelve Steps were businesspeople, so it was only natural they'd hit upon the metaphor of taking stock. Well, a tally of only the damaged merchandise would leave a shop owner with an incomplete picture. Now that we've probed our shortcomings, it's time to make an inventory of our strengths. Letting go of our character defects, the goal of the next few Steps, will be easier when we know what we want to hold on to instead.

We've talked about how most of our resentments and fears resulted from warped instincts. As we became more and more self-centered in our addiction, our natural defense mechanisms got hijacked. But underneath all of those problematic behaviors there were simple human instincts. And they weren't all bad! A catalog of our assets might begin with a list (we're crystal meth addicts; we love lists) based on those same instincts. We feel remorse for our shortcomings, those character defects of pride, anger, greed, gluttony, lust, envy, and sloth. But we can be grateful for times we've had a healthy self-esteem and the courage to stand up for ourselves; when we've known how to work hard, pay our bills, and maybe save a bit of money; when we've felt motivated or inspired by others' accomplishments; when we've been passionate about life and passionately uninhibited with the people we love.

STEP FOUR

Or our sponsors might ask us to look at all our most glaring defects and name their opposites. If we have a tendency to get angry, we think back to times we've been forgiving and calm. If we can sometimes be conceited, we remember other moments when we were humble. If we've cheated, we ask when we did the honest thing instead. If we're prone to gossip, we recount times when we were kind and praising.

Here's another popular approach. We look at our moral inventory and take the 12 most persistent character defects (if we have that many) and list two assets for each one. Two for each defect, period—this is nonnegotiable. We're experts at criticizing ourselves but have a hard time acknowledging our good points. In the moral inventory, we've written about actual life events where our defects cropped up; now we do the opposite and write a sentence or two about life events where we needed our assets. Just as the moral inventory was only a list, so too is this. We don't analyze ourselves or describe our personality; we just give concrete examples.

A lot of us resist writing about our assets, much less talking about them. We don't mind telling people what a piece of shit we are, but looking someone in the eye and saying that we're kind or funny or loving is impossible. But an honest inventory requires listing everything—the bad and the good. We need to remember why we're worth saving.

TAKING STOCK

The inventory process is a remarkable thing. We've learned that we ourselves are responsible for a lot of our own emotional distress. As the Serenity Prayer says, we strive to accept the things we cannot change—but we also want courage to change the things we can. And making drama for ourselves and others is definitely a thing we can change!

We started by thinking of others as enemies and ourselves as victims. We noted our normal human instincts

THE TWELVE STEPS

and described how they'd been thwarted. Next, we turned our attention, maybe for the first time, to our side of the street, and acknowledged our own role in our difficulties. We named the character defects we most often resort to. Then we held our deepest fears up to the light, exposing most of them as false. We followed that by detailing all our overlooked assets and crafted a beautiful list of spiritual principles to live by.

We've done a thorough investigation of our inner workings. In the next few Steps, we'll use this information to focus on changing behaviors that get us into trouble, setting aside old habits, and bringing out our better selves. But before we move on, we need to examine in more detail one area of life that gives most of us trouble: sex.

STEP FOUR

THE TWELVE STEPS

WHAT ABOUT SEX?

Let's stop right here for a moment. The inventory process has taken most of us into a part of our lives that gives us a lot of trouble: sex, where our instincts, anxieties, and assets get especially tangled up. Fear not! In Crystal Meth Anonymous, we spend a lot of time on this topic, especially in early recovery. And it's time well spent—eventually, we're no longer terrified to climb into bed.

It's not that the rules are any different for these relationships; resentment and fear are the source of most our difficulties here, just like in the rest of our lives. But sex can be especially disorienting for many of us—compulsive, obsessive sexual behavior was often a major feature of our disease. And the unmanageability we wrote about in Step One may have included a good deal of shame and guilt about where our drug-driven sex took us. We will need to cultivate a new attitude toward intimacy. We call this our sexual ideal.

SOBER SEX

By the time we get to Step Four, some of us are having sex again—and experiencing all the feelings, good and bad, that come with it. Maybe we're rebuilding the physical side of a relationship that took a beating while we were using. Maybe we're dating for the first time as a sober person and pursuing pleasure without drugs or alcohol. Or maybe we're enjoying playing the field with a clear head. A lot of us may not be having sex at all; either we've had traumatic experiences and aren't ready for intimacy yet, or we binged on it in active addiction and we're treasuring the new intimacy with ourselves we've discovered in abstinence.

Sex is much more exciting—more satisfying and intimate—when we're in our right mind, but we don't get to that awareness overnight. For many of us, sex just doesn't feel sober at first. Getting physical reminds us of using: Our brain may understand that our chemsex lifestyle was all about the chems and not really the sex; but the wiring to the rest of our body is still tangled up. When we feel shaky, we ask the following: Am I actually getting high? Do I find myself wishing I was? Are my partners high? If it feels like our behavior isn't consistent with staying clean, and we start fantasizing about crystal, we take the suggestion to slow down and not force anything. If we think we need meth or weed or poppers to really let go, we probably aren't ready to really let go.

Many of us feared that our fixation on drug-driven sex had robbed us of the ability to have a healthy sex life—but this isn't true. Deep intimacy is a possibility for all of us. We just need more clarity and a bit of healing time. One fellow describes early sobriety this way: He used to go from bed to bed chasing a high; now he goes from meeting to meeting chasing recovery. We reach out to our sponsor and other fellows we trust for nonjudgmental guidance; on this topic more than most, we've found it's key to keep an honest channel open with the people who have our back. And we lean hard into Steps One, Two, and Three. We are powerless over drugs—we have to accept that and turn it over to our Higher Power, even in the bedroom. We don't pick up no matter what, even if that means not having sex for a while. It may seem insane, but we can survive a few months without sex.

A SEXUAL INVENTORY

Most of our sponsors suggest we do one last inventory, examining a part of life that seems to defy rational analysis. In bed, our biological instincts collide with our family or cultural upbringing, our sharpest resentments overlap with our fondest memories, and our biggest assets bump into our deepest fears. And our time in active addiction certainly didn't clarify any of this for us.

Simply put, sex is very, very confusing.

Our sponsors tell us to start by looking over the love and sex relationships we've already written about in our inventory. We note times when we let people treat us poorly and times when we ourselves could have behaved better. Next we think about other encounters, experiences that didn't necessarily generate any resentment on our side but left us feeling uncomfortable just the same. We ask: Where were we selfish, dishonest, or inconsiderate? When did we unjustifiably arouse jealousy, suspicion, or bitterness? Have we been hurtful or abusive to anyone? Have we objectified partners, reducing them to their attributes and overlooking their humanity? Have we allowed them to dehumanize us? Did we walk right into situations where we knew we'd get hurt? Can we name the fears that motivated our warped behaviors toward others and ourselves?

Many of us have been subjected to sexual abuse or harassment, sometimes long ago. And we probably described those incidents in our inventory of resentments. Some of us have normalized our traumas and learned to disassociate in the bedroom. Others of us, clinging to our pain, are terrified of entering into any relationships at all. When Step Four says we look at our part in everything, it isn't telling us we are responsible for being victimized. But it does encourage us to take an active role in our healing. If we've been harassed or assaulted and need assistance from the authorities or doctors or therapists, we get that outside help when we are ready. In recovery, we learn to show up for ourselves.

We also learn to see our good sides, those assets we've talked about. Now our sponsors tell us to write about connections that worked well—times when we were passionate, considerate, and honest with our partners. What experiences left us feeling great—not just sensually, but emotionally and spiritually? When were we generous? When were we open and truthful? When were we caring and thoughtful? When did we show impartiality and acceptance? Who did we nurture? Who nurtured our senses and spirit? When did we feel harmony and trust?

We are beginning to develop what the program calls a sexual ideal, our own spiritual approach to intimacy and relationships. This inventory of healthy and unhealthy sexual experiences will give us a good idea of the kinds of intimate connections we may want to avoid—and seek out.

BUILDING A SEXUAL IDEAL

When our sponsors ask us about our sexual ideal, we may be confused. Are they talking about our ideal partner? By all means, they tell us, we can give that as much thought as we like. But the ideal they're talking about is much more important: What sort of partner do *we* want to be?

Part of the answer is in our sexual inventory. Looking over it, many of us realize we may owe people amends. As with other resentments, our sponsors tell us not to agonize about that—there will be time to try to make things right at Step Nine. For now, the important thing is to identify things that didn't work well for us or our partners. Rather than wallowing in guilt, we focus on cultivating deeper empathy and mindfulness and commit to behaving differently. We spend even more time on the other side of the ledger, describing experiences that left us feeling sensually and spiritually great. Thinking back on healthy connections and open-hearted relationships gives us a good idea of what we might seek as part of our sexual ideal.

Then comes the hardest question: How do we feel about ourselves? If we aren't hurting anyone, what we do in bed is nobody else's business. But what if we're hurting ourselves? A lot of us feel guilty about the sex we have—or worse, we feel shame, believing we're inherently flawed for having physical

WHAT ABOUT SEX?

needs and desires. This toxic sort of self-loathing is planted in most of us when we're very small, passed on by families or churches or schools. And unhealthy or abusive relationships may have intensified the feeling that our fundamental urges are abnormal. Now that we're sober, we have a chance to put these feelings behind us. It's not easy—many of us also get help from a therapist to untangle these issues.

Next we ask: How do we treat ourselves? Does our sex life affect our health? Does it mess with our sleep pattern and energy level? Does the time we invest in fantasizing about and planning for sex crowd out other parts of life? Are we using sex compulsively to suppress feelings or avoid responsibilities? If our interests are damaging our health or well-being, we take a long look at that. If we can't learn to honor our fun, naughty side without hurting ourselves or others, we'll only perpetuate feelings of guilt and shame.

We can be as powerless over sex as we are over drugs, seeking the "high" it gives us. And it can create just as much unmanageability in our lives, damaging our physical well-being and putting obstacles in the way of truly intimate relationships. Our sponsors have useful insights; they've had their share of experiences good and bad with sex and romance. And some of us, deciding we have a sex addiction as well as a drug problem, decide to pursue sexual sobriety as well. As with any obstacle, we have the willingness now to go further and seek outside help to overcome it.

Writing out our sexual ideal usually starts with the proposition that, now that we're sober, we try to behave in a way that feels spiritually sound. We've learned by now that the unpleasant feelings that come with transactional self-centered sex—guilt, jealousy, low self-esteem, shame—can lead us back to crystal. We can clearly describe attachments that didn't work out so well, as well as connections that deepened our feelings of love for others and ourselves.

We aren't used to thinking of sex from a spiritual angle, so it helps to get started with a list of defenses and attributes: We considered the value of dishonesty vs. honesty; selfishness vs. generosity; distrust vs. trust; secretiveness vs. disclosure; pride vs. humility; dismissiveness vs. empathy. How might these principles find their way into the bedroom? For more perspective, we ask fellows we trust to tell us about their ideals. They're happy to share with us.

And when we're ready, we ask our Higher Power for the courage to write down our own. With all of these ideas and ideals in mind, we might ask ourselves: No matter what turns me on, do I take care of myself and my partner? Do they treat me with respect, honor, and affection? Do I treat them the same? If I have relationships that are strictly sexual, do I honor those partners as whole people? How would I feel if I ran into them on the street? Would I be happy to stop for coffee?

Listening as we craft our ideal, our sponsors offer encouragement and point us to a clear future without guilt, shame, or remorse. Most of us come up with three or four spiritual guidelines and do our best to follow them. We don't use the Steps to beat ourselves up, and the same goes with our sexual ideal. If we should fall short in some way—and it will happen, hormones being what they are—we take it as an opportunity for more growth and reflection.

We've said that there are as many concepts of a Higher Power in CMA as there are fellows, and the same goes for our sexual ideals. This is a very sensitive subject that each of us approaches from our own very personal perspective—a perspective that will undoubtedly change, by the way. We aren't etching a law into stone. Our sexual ideal will evolve as we do.

VULNERABILITY

Sex is sacred. When we get naked, we're just about as vulnerable as we can be in life. Some emotional discomfort is the

WHAT ABOUT SEX?

price of intense pleasure and nurturing connections. It can be terrifying. But if we're clear about what sober sex means for us; if we've done a thorough inventory of our past relationships; and if we go into encounters with a solid sense of how we want to behave, there is nothing more exciting.

Now we need to find the courage to share everything we've learned as we've made our inventory of resentments, character defects, fears, and assets—and meditated on a sexual ideal—with another human being and our Higher Power. In fact, most of us began having that conversation as we wrote it all out. We've painted a complete picture of all the wonderful and not-so-wonderful parts of our psyche. Are we ready to show it to someone else?

STEP

Admitted to God, to ourselves and to another human being the exact nature of our wrongs.

Searching through all the painful twists in our history, all our secrets and sorrows, is hard. Our suffering is all we know; it takes courage to acknowledge our own role in past conflicts and continuing resentments, to catalog our defects, and to describe our deepest fears. We're used to looking at everything through a dark, self-centered lens, but putting it away, we begin to see the world clearly for the first time.

We've done this before, in Step One, when we accepted the objective truth of our situation. Still, though we might be more and more comfortable facing reality in our meditations or journals, finding the words to share all of this out loud with another human being will take a lot of courage. But we'll need to talk about our discomfort if we want to find relief. Sunlight makes the best disinfectant, as they say, and that's the essence of Step Five: We're leading someone into the dark, dusty corners of our past, and pointing out all the clutter we've hidden away.

IDENTIFICATION

If finding the truth was the point of Step Four, sharing it was the essence of Step Five. Who could we trust to hear our inventory? In some cases, we chose to confide in someone who wasn't in the fellowship, a family friend, doctor, or spiritual guide. But over the decades, for the vast majority of us, the person we were willing to share our Fifth Step with was our sponsor. And that only made sense.

This was someone we'd learned we could count on when we were first counting days and saw how their sensible suggestions were helping us stay sober a day at a time. When we shared our First Step with them that trust deepened. It was easier to find the humility to describe our humiliation, knowing they'd suffered in crystal addiction just as we had. (Some of their stories were even crazier than ours!) They trusted us with their confidences, just as we trusted them with ours. Our sponsors respect our privacy—they aren't the sort to pass along secrets, gossip about fellows, or point fingers. Whoever we chose to share the Fifth Step with, we had to trust them.

In Step Five, we laid bare the terrible things that had happened to us and, more important, the terrible things we'd done. Difficult as this work was, most of us felt relieved. We spilled our shame and pain out to another person, and they didn't reject us or judge us at all. Sizing up the whole sorry storehouse, they more often said, "I can totally identify!" Without blinking, they described their own selfishness and their own broken relationships. Then they shared the beautiful promise that we could heal just as they had, by letting go of some of our old notions. They showed us love and compassion, telling us they'd been in many similar, embarrassing situations, made many of the same mistakes, felt lots of the same regrets.

Finally, someone understood us. We may have seen our sponsors as authority figures, and where the program and the Steps are concerned, they certainly were. But now we saw them as our peers: They'd recovered from the same disease that had destroyed our lives and gone through exactly this process themselves. It had a tremendous effect on our recovery, asking for suggestions and taking them. It helped us to surrender even more of our ego. We found the courage to lay out our pain for someone; and then we followed their suggestions to begin the healing process.

CLARITY

Some of us wondered why we needed to describe "the exact nature of our wrongs" to God and to ourselves—hadn't we already done that in Step Four? Weren't we admitting our resentments and character defects to ourselves as we wrote? And wasn't the universe listening? Yes, and

WHAT ABOUT SEX?

yes, depending on how we conceived of our Higher Power. But we couldn't admit something to ourselves if we didn't completely understand it, and that's another reason we needed Step Five.

As we said in Step Four, most of us checked in with our sponsors as we worked on our moral inventory, and we needed their help to debunk our fears and highlight our assets, as well. Our Fifth Step began, in other words, the moment we asked for guidance. Our sponsors had the one thing we couldn't provide ourselves, no matter how fearless and searching we were—they had an objective perspective. They could give us clarity.

Few of us could really see "the exact nature of our wrongs." We either believed nothing was ever our fault—or we were sure we had caused all the world's heartache. Our sponsors helped us right-size our pain, gently turning our attention to the role we'd played in causing our own diffi-culties. Or, where we had marinated in guilty feelings so long that we imagined we were monsters, they helped restore some context, dispelling our self-loathing. None of us was quite as good or bad as we thought we were.

How we did this work varied from relationship to relationship—as we've said, there are countless approaches to each Step. But most of us needed some help from our sponsors in naming our character defects, so we could begin assessing the flawed coping strategies we'd relied on. Contemplating our past trauma and shame, some of us had a tendency to spiral into dark places; our sponsors proved invaluable, patiently helping us diffuse these moods. Usually they did this by shifting our focus to a fear inventory, show-ing us that many of the ideas we had about the world and ourselves were utterly wrong. If it's a relief to share our secrets with someone else, it's a pleasure to unravel the false stories we've been telling ourselves.

And finally, they were eager to help us recognize the good sides of our character. Guiding us through the first four Steps, our sponsors had gotten just about our whole story. They knew our shortcomings inside and out, but also our strengths. They could describe attributes we weren't able to see: when we'd been brave and strong, honest and responsible, generous and loving.

Whether we checked in often as we wrote Step Four or sat down and talked through the whole thing in one afternoon, it was the same for all of us. We couldn't admit the truth to ourselves until we'd shared it with another human being—because half the time we couldn't quite see it.

ACCOUNTABILITY AND INTEGRITY

The feeling of identification we felt the first time we heard other recovering addicts share their stories deepened with this Step. But something even more profound happened. Finally, we were willing to be accountable to another person. Given that the program is built on community, service, and identification, it's intriguing that Step Five is the only place that specifically mentions getting help from "another human being." That's how important this idea of accountability is for us addicts. We cannot answer only to ourselves.

As we've said, we wouldn't have been able to clearly find our way through our defenses, fears, and assets on our own anyway. We asked our sponsors for help, and they freely gave it. A lot of us felt shy. This was a lot to ask of someone; what were we giving them? A lot, they told us: purpose, confidence, camaraderie—and above all, that same accountability we now felt. Because they couldn't guide us through the inventory process (and on toward letting go of our character defects and making amends) without redoing it, at least mentally, themselves.

WHAT ABOUT SEX?

We hadn't answered to anyone in many years. There was a kind of relief in it. Finally, someone knew where the bodies were buried. It was bad enough when we were using, knowing we'd disappointed ourselves. Now that we were accountable to our sponsor—and probably other fellows, too—we wouldn't be able to let ourselves down without others knowing. Someone in the fellowship was rooting for us to stay sober; we'd gone through our inventory with them, and they'd shown they were available to help us tackle almost any challenge that gave us trouble.

Being so thoroughly honest with ourselves and another human being brought a new spiritual awareness. As we shared all of this with our sponsor—and accepted their help in understanding our resentments, defects, and fears—we were also sharing it with our Higher Power. But most of us took the wording of the Step at face value: We admitted our wrongs and fears and assets to God in an overt way. How we communicated with our H.P. was of course up to us; some of us went to a special place to have that conversation with the God of our understanding. To nurture the connection, many of us prayed and meditated. We asked our Higher Power for help revealing our true selves, the good and bad, so we could make progress in our recovery. Many of us asked for forgiveness, as well, and something even more important: a better way forward. We already had the willingness to change—we'd demonstrated that by reaching out for the support of our sponsor and the fellowship.

Most important, we asked for acceptance. With our sponsor's help, we finally showed ourselves some healing compassion. Looking at our history, we saw that there weren't any deal-breakers, after all. We feel relieved about the past, and hopeful for the future. Thinking back on his Fifth Step, one old-timer says, "I began to see how truly good I am. You couldn't stop me from doing the rest of the Steps!"

We finally had some integrity, a code of conduct to follow even when no one was watching. Experiencing this inner transformation, most of us became almost joyful. We were no longer embarrassed about our past. We weren't afraid of unexpected encounters. The compassion we began to show ourselves now extended to others. We were willing to pull our own weight in a world we'd shunned—and better still, that world seemed eager to take us back. With this spiritual breakthrough, anything felt possible.

THE NEXT RIGHT THING

We naturally feel a sense of accomplishment at this point in the Steps. Doing the moral inventory, we began to see our part in our own suffering, the many ways we've either contributed to conflicts in the past or continue to hold on to grudges today. Looking at our fears, we learned that we really don't need them to keep us safe. We now see clearly the forces that drive the way we react in any given situation. Cataloging the assets we've long overlooked and describing the spiritual principles we're bringing into our lives, we realized we have most of the tools we need to solve any problem.

We've searched our souls and shared our secrets with our Higher Power and another human being, and all that heavy lifting has left us feeling a lot lighter. With our sponsor's guidance, we've even come up with a sexual ideal to work toward in our most intimate relationships. Possibly for the first time in our lives, we have a clear, commonsense way to handle difficulties from the past and present.

A lot of us feel like we should get some kind of prize for finishing Four and Five. Our only reward is to move on to the next Steps—but we're usually pretty excited to do it. Six and Seven offer us the chance to live without all of our resentments and fears and to cultivate our existing assets and build new ones. Now we will begin putting our design for living into practice.

WHAT ABOUT SEX?

STEP

Were entirely ready to have God remove all these defects of character.

We've combed through our past and zeroed in on our conflicts and resentments. We've taken a long look at our fears and developed a new appreciation of our emotional assets. We've paid special attention to our intimate relationships and begun to develop a sexual ideal to live by. We have done a lot of work, examining our whole psyche from a fresh perspective.

Not surprisingly, most of us end the inventory feeling a bit preoccupied with our exes, old bosses, and former friends. We want to rush out and apologize! Not so fast, the program tells us. We aren't ready to make amends yet. Whatever the thing was—cheating, stealing, lying, avoiding, disparaging— we need to be sure we aren't going to do it again. Once more, we're reminded that the Steps come in order for a reason: We're building a house; each brick rests on the one below it.

Yes, we're sober now, and yes, we know today exactly who we've hurt and how. But the character defects we've uncovered do not belong to the past. Maladapted as they are, they've become our instinctual defenses, the way we react when we're threatened or cornered. Being clean won't automatically stop us from behaving badly. We're likely to turn to our character defects again and again. Don N., who helped start Crystal Meth Anonymous in the 1990s, had a salty way of summing up recovery: "Quit doing drugs and stop being an asshole." In the next pair of Steps, Six and Seven, we begin the long process of not acting like an asshole. If we're lucky, we'll keep at it until the day we die.

CHARACTER DEFENSES

In the early years of Twelve Step recovery, people didn't spend a lot of time on Six and Seven. At the end of Step Five, a sponsor might say: "Well, you did a lot of damage. Are you ready to be rid of all those destructive traits?" If the sponsee said yes—and who wouldn't?—they'd be sent somewhere to pray on it, and presto, they'd arrive at Step Eight. But it's usually not that simple. Over the years, we've learned we need to spend a little more time examining our default behaviors and becoming entirely ready to have them removed. By now, most of us have powerful evidence that our obsession to use can be lifted, but as for all of our *other* problems? The fears and character defects that keep us in conflict with the world can continue to torment us for a long, long time.

Some say Six and Seven are where we really begin to grow up. Looking back over the inventory we shared with our sponsor, we might note that we have a history of angry outbursts or rash correspondence. Maybe we're prone to gossiping or telling little lies. Perhaps we've shrunk from relationships, having a fear of intimacy; we're more comfortable objectifying anonymous sex partners. Fearing poverty, we may have been too scared to take risks that might pay off in our career. Whatever our shortcomings are, they won't magically vanish. They may be warped and destructive, but they're a part of us. It feels unnatural on a gut level to let them go.

Cowering in fear, lashing out, being quietly manipulative: We learned all these strategies long before we ever touched drugs and alcohol. And they may have worked in a backward way. That's why many of us prefer to call these traits character defenses instead of defects—we needed them to survive. If we never take any risks, we'll never get rejected. If we're often angry, people will learn to stay out of our way. If we're devious and manipulative, we may indeed get the things we think we want from people. And if we never care to look at these things, so what? We find a strange comfort trapped in the hypnotic grasp of self-pity.

The problem is that, a lot of the time, these self-serving strategies don't truly serve us anymore. We're safely isolated, righteously rageful, or shrewdly passive-aggressive, but also perpetually lonely and tragically unfulfilled. Doing things

STEP SIX

our old way doesn't work so well now we're sober. We believe if we follow our familiar instincts, they will eventually lead us back into the despair of addiction. We came to CMA because we were willing to try something different. To take a new approach. We learned all of our old instincts in reaction to old experiences. Changing them will require not only a new approach, but also new experiences. And patience.

ACTING AS IF

If we could get rid of our shortcomings on our own, we'd have done so a long time ago. That's why Step Six doesn't say we *let go* of our character defects; it only suggests that we become willing to have God remove them. We need help. Actually asking our Higher Power to remove them comes in the next Step—for now, we're merely getting "ready." How on Earth do we do that?

Most of us start by considering our defects and fears and asking what their opposites are. As it happens, we just made a detailed list of all our warped instincts in Step Four and shared about them in Step Five. Many of us take that specific list and, with our sponsor's help, write out their opposites. Could we be gentle instead of aggressive? Humble vs. conceited? Confident vs. insecure? Diligent vs. lazy? Faithful vs. disloyal? In our prayers and meditations, we ask: Are we willing to stop doing X, Y, or Z? Are we willing to try A, B, or C instead?

The inventory process was all about our history, but we're not looking at the past anymore. We are peering into the present. And as we go about our sober lives, a lot of us are embarrassed to realize we still do some of this stuff! Well, we are human, after all. We're not going to unlearn a lifetime of unhealthy habits in an instant.

To help us along, our sponsors might ask us to notice throughout the day when we're feeling uncomfortable or

THE TWELVE STEPS

upset and identify whatever character defects are flaring up. Many of them suggested we do a nightly recap: Where did things go south? Our shortcomings always appear when we're operating on instinct. Maybe we snapped at a coworker. Or gossiped about someone in our home group. Perhaps we didn't answer the phone when our parents called. Or we flirted with someone we shouldn't have. Our sponsors might ask: How did losing our temper serve us? How did running down so-and-so help anything? What did we communicate by avoiding Mom and Dad? Will sexting with that totally unavailable person bring us any closer to intimacy? More important, they ask, *What could we have done instead?*

The answers are usually obvious: We could have taken a deep breath and stepped away from the argument. We could have said something nice about so-and-so and changed the subject. We could have survived a 10-minute talk with Mom. That racy text we sent back to a flirtatious newcomer could have been a helpful program message instead.

Stopping ourselves in the middle of a reaction is especially hard. Knowing we're often going to be confused about our impulses, our sponsors teach us to practice "restraint of tongue and pen." If we feel a powerful urge to write or say something, we ask ourselves three questions: Does whatever it is need to be said? Does it need to be said by me? Does it need to be said by me right now?

Watching ourselves in this process, we start to develop a list of not only our defects or challenges, but also their opposites. It's time to try taking contrary actions. To catch the impulse as it's coming over us, take a deep breath, and… do the opposite. We call this acting as if. When we'd normally have a judgmental reaction to something, we try to be accepting instead. When we feel anger rising inside, we strive to stay calm. When we're about to give in to some old, self-centered impulse, we ask instead how we might be of service.

We developed all our coping strategies honestly; setting them aside and taking contrary actions may feel perversely dishonest at first. But there's nothing false about it. We are visualizing the things we want to do—the person we want to be—just as a dancer, gymnast, or ice skater eyes a difficult leap they're about to make. Acting as if our Higher Power has removed our defects and provided the assets we need, we grow more and more confident. Soon we're able to gracefully stick the landing.

We "fake it 'til we make it," and before we know it, we start reporting things like this to our sponsor: We wrote a vicious email to our coworker but then deleted it. We purposely asked that irritating guy at our home group how his day was—turns out he's also a huge basketball fan. We got up 10 minutes early and made the bed, and it felt so great to come home to a neat room! We let our partner choose the next show to watch, even though we think zombies are preposterous. And so on. We act our way into sober living—and someday we're pleasantly surprised to realize we aren't acting any longer.

LETTING GO OF FEAR

Perhaps the biggest obstacle to our freedom—greater than any character defect—is fear. We're not talking about the useful sort of fear, our instinct for self-preservation. In recovery, we've even developed a new one: the healthy fear of relapse. We don't climb trees in a lightning storm, dive into a pool of sharks, or hang out in our old using den.

Most of our day-to-day fears, though, really aren't so helpful. We're convinced we will fail at our job. We're too anxious to go on dates. We're terrified that some financial catastrophe or unforeseen malady is just around the corner. Yes, bad things happen, even to good people. But when our sponsors talked over our fears with us in Step Five, they helped us see that usually our expectations of dire outcomes rarely came to pass. That's what FEAR is, they said: False Evidence Appearing Real.

If we're doing a nightly meditation, we might ask then if any fears have gotten the better of us. Did anything today trigger our old anxieties—about money, our reputation, our love life? Our sponsors will remind us that somehow we have so far survived every sort of setback. Chiefly, we're getting sober today—not that long ago, we thought our life had ended in a hopeless dead end.

One way to bring this home is to note our successes along with our stumbles. What challenges did we successfully meet today? How are we doing with opportunities? Are we standing up for ourselves, taking a chance with a new acquaintance or job? A wise fellow likes to say, "Fear is just excitement without the breath. So take a breath and get excited!" We ask ourselves: What happened today that was new and exciting?

WILLINGNESS

From time to time, all of us will throw up our hands. What Step Six seems to ask of us is simply impossible. We will never be perfect.

No, we won't ever be perfect, but we are changing. Again—aren't we clean today? Not too long ago, weren't we positive that we'd never be able to put down crystal meth and all other mind-altering substances? If hopeless addicts can perform this daily miracle, what else can we achieve? If we stay honest, open-minded, and above all willing, we can be relieved of all sorts of problems, just as we've been relieved of our addiction.

To help us become entirely ready to let go of our character defects, we might spend some time looking at our list and meditating on how those old strategies are no longer

STEP SIX

useful—how they no longer serve us—and how we're learning to take better actions. We affirm that we don't want to reserve a place for our old coping mechanisms in the future. And we imagine what life would look like without them: What would our relationships look like? What would our job and workday be like? Wouldn't we be more serene if we didn't feel so disturbed all the time? This kind of introspection can help us become *entirely ready* to ask our Higher Power to remove our old fears and defense mechanisms.

Our fellows taught us to be gentle with ourselves when we get triggered to use. Accepting that we're addicts helps us take action to get through bouts of craving. In the same way, we're not hard on ourselves when we fall short in our quest to be a generally less disagreeable human being. One of the mantras of recovery is "progress, not perfection." We may not be perfect angels today, but we probably aren't deplorable demons either. It's not easy to unlearn lifelong patterns—if we're one percent better today than we were yesterday, that's progress. It's all practice. We just need to hang on to one thing—our willingness to grow, to keep on practicing—and we'll be surprised before we know it at how much we are changing.

We are taking concrete actions to overcome our shortcomings, setting aside our selfish impulses and doing the opposite thing. Changing is a terrifying prospect for an addict, yet we're more and more willing to do just that. We are becoming "entirely ready" to be rid of all our obstacles. But to really do it, we're going to need a hand. We didn't stop using on our own, and neither will we set aside all our other self-destructive behaviors. That's why we need Step Seven. We've got to find the humility to ask for help.

STEP

Humbly asked God to remove our shortcomings.

In Step Six, we became willing to live without resorting to our old coping strategies. We learned how to act as if, to try different approaches to our difficulties. If we're willing to keep at it, reminding ourselves to pause and take a breath when we meet a challenge—to proceed thoughtfully instead of reacting out of fear or spite—eventually we're no longer acting. Our former approach is simply gone. Our maladapted instincts and ingrained fears may return from time to time, but they no longer define who we are. If we can really live in Step Six, being mindful of our actions and earnestly attempting more constructive behaviors, we really can change our instincts. It sure sounds simple!

Well, coming up against our old instincts again and again (and again), we realize it's not as easy as it seems. None of us succeeds at this entirely. In recovery, we judge ourselves by actions, not intentions, and there are lots of days when our heart is in the right place, but the rest of us doesn't follow. Our mantra remains "progress, not perfection." And time and again, we get rudely reminded of just how imperfect we are. Identifying our fears and character defects and then learning to take contrary actions instead of succumbing to our worst instincts is hard work. We will often fall short of the ideals we're cultivating. We must be exceedingly patient, because the awful truth is this: We cannot completely remove our shortcomings without help. That's where Step Seven comes in.

HUMILITY

The realization that we'll never be perfect doesn't discourage us. Today we understand there is no magic spell that can whisk away our shortcomings and problems. Many of us thought crystal meth was some kind of wonder drug—offering a perfect escape from troubles and challenges and immunity from the rules of real life—but hitting bottom

THE TWELVE STEPS

completely humbled our grand fantasies of absolute control. Getting sober, we experience a lot of pain and discomfort. Without it, we might never find true humility.

Some of us get confused by that word. Feeling *humiliated* is a thing we know well from hitting bottom on crystal meth—in our addiction, we experienced all sorts of suffering, sorrow, and remorse. Learning *humility* is something else entirely: getting a clear, unvarnished view of ourselves. Humility is a precious attribute we strive to cultivate, the antidote to the self-destructive grandiosity or toxic self-loathing that fueled our using. If we can accept, without shame, our good and bad sides, we can really begin to grow.

We're in luck. The meticulous examination of our instincts we did in Step Six carries with it still more humility and brings us closer to our Higher Power. Whatever God is, it clearly isn't us. At Step Seven, we freely admit this and appeal to the God of our understanding for help. We humbly ask our Higher Power to do what we cannot— remove any obstacles to being connected and useful and happy.

Asking our Higher Power for help doesn't mean we give up and give in to our instincts. Where they continue to get us into trouble, we ask again (and again and again) to be teachable: Every impulsive reaction is a fresh opportunity to gain more wisdom. We will always have another chance to act as if—to let the impulse go and do something that would serve us better.

We can turn to the spiritual opposites we developed when we described our defects, fears, and assets as gentle alternatives to the flaws we used to cling to. These higher qualities aren't a bludgeon to beat ourselves up with; they're guiding stars to help us get back on course. This compassionate way of redirecting our intentions is much more useful than the shaming

STEP SEVEN

perfectionism we used to resort to—self-shame is just another defect we're letting go of as we become our better selves.

Step Seven is a bit of a wake-up call. Being human means making mistakes—there's just no cure for it. We can only accept our flaws and keep working a day at a time to overcome them. Humility doesn't come easily to us addicts. We're much more familiar with humiliation, having gone up in flames when we hit bottom. In recovery we find new strength in accepting our powerlessness and new liberty in surrendering our willpower. In CMA our degradation gives way to dignity.

ASKING OUR HIGHER POWER

Consulting with our sponsors, we decide when we're ready. We choose a place where the connection with our Higher Power feels strong. If we're religious, it might be a church or temple. If we're atheist or agnostic, we might go to our favorite museum or a quiet park or a windy beach. Some of us do it sitting with our sponsor at the kitchen table. Where we go to formally do Step Seven is a deeply personal choice—the place isn't as important as the practice.

We can use whatever words we like, of course, but many of us reiterate our humility by borrowing this prayer from the Big Book of Alcoholics Anonymous, which millions of addicts before us have used:

> *My Creator, I am now willing that you should have all of me, good and bad. I pray that you now remove from me every single defect of character which stands in the way of my usefulness to you and my fellows. Grant me strength, as I go out from here, to do your bidding.*

If our concept of a Higher Power is less of a deity and more of a higher ideal, we might write a prayer that helps

THE TWELVE STEPS

us call out each character defect and remember the spiritual opposite we're developing. Something like:

> *I declare my willingness to let go of my character defect of _____. I recognize it's no longer serving the greater good, so I let it be removed. I'm now willing to replace it with _____, so I can be more useful to myself and the world.*

The Step tells us only that "we humbly asked God to remove our shortcomings," not that "we had God take away our shortcomings." Our progress may be slow, but each stumble is a "teachable moment"—a chance for character building and reflection. Our Higher Power operates on its schedule, not ours. And sometimes it seems like character building is all it expects of us.

Like most of the Steps, in other words, Seven isn't a onetime deal. Recognizing how hard it will be on any given day to take the next right action, many of us start our morning with a few minutes of meditation, or we say a short prayer to this effect:

> *Today, help me set aside the defects of character that block my recovery. Help me take actions that will serve me, those around me, and the universe better.*

We set our daily intention and then follow through. And if we get to the end of the day and need to ask the universe (once again!) to help with our short temper or our fear of failure, so be it. In active addiction, we stumbled through life denying we had any problems. Now we humbly admit that we still need help—to stay sober to start with, but also to quit gossiping or self-sabotaging or whatever.

You'll often hear people talk about "the grace of God," or say this or that will happen "with a little luck." But you may also hear this mind-bender: "God is a verb." Our spirituality in recovery isn't passive. We find our Higher Power in the actions we take; every time we do the next right thing, we're building up our connection with it. Cultivating willingness and humility, we're putting ourselves in the path of grace and making ourselves available to enjoy all the luck the universe can offer.

A BLANK CANVAS

In the grips of our running-away disease, we spent our days chasing insane fantasies. In recovery, we're learning not just to tolerate reality, but also to treasure it. Steps Four and Five were difficult; but now we have a way to overcome the fears and resentments that caused us so much pain. Six and Seven are even more challenging—none of us likes finding out just how deeply ingrained our character defects are. Letting those familiar behaviors go may seem impossible.

Behind our old habits, we've been holding on to some even older fears we're perversely attached to. But the day will come when we let them go: We find ourselves in some typically tricky situation; instead of reacting in our usual way, we "act as if" and do something else; and amazingly, the world does not end. Seeing that our fears no longer have to dictate our actions is liberating. We become more willing to model new behaviors and more willing to humbly ask for help. Soon we begin to glimpse a remarkable new person— the person we might become.

Every one of us is a blank canvas. We have no idea who we might someday be and what we might achieve. But for the first time, not knowing what might be coming in the future doesn't terrify us. We were never able to think our way into right actions—we have to "move a muscle to change a thought." With the help of our Higher Power, day by day, our spiritual muscles grow stronger. Our thinking changes completely. The blank canvas stretches in surprising directions and fills with delightful, unexpected colors. In recovery, whatever we dream of doing, we can go for it!

Striving to set aside the flawed way we used to operate, we're also no longer afraid of the past. In the next two Steps, we'll finally repair the damage we've caused in our using career and elsewhere, so we can live today with a clear conscience— and face that unknown future with a clear mind.

STEP SEVEN

STEP

Made a list of all persons we had harmed and became willing to make amends to them all.

STEP EIGHT

In Steps Four and Five, we surveyed the debris of our lives and acknowledged just how much of the destruction was of our own making. In Six and Seven, we recognized our warped instincts and began the lifelong process of developing new ones. We're less liable to fall into the emotional messes that used to lead us to relapse; and when things do explode, as they still will, we're equipped with tools to make the situation right. We are just about ready to go out into the world. Only one obstacle remains: We've faced the past—are we ready to face the people from it? That's our job in the next pair of Steps, Eight and Nine.

Our sponsors tell us to begin by looking again at our inventory from Step Four. Here was a catalog of most of the people we'd wronged, and notes about exactly what we needed to attempt to repair. Some of these people and institutions may not carry over to Step Eight; we have nothing to fix, apart from our own resentments. On the other hand, we may have harmed people we *don't* really resent. Our focus here isn't so much on our feelings about a situation—we're just taking stock of any damage we caused. What needs repairing? That's what "amend" means: to restore or put right, to correct or make restitution.

It also describes sewing something back together, which sums up well what we're about to do. We don't snap our fingers and—presto!—it's done. Making amends is more like tugging a needle and thread through a torn pair of jeans. It requires concentration and focus. Do we have the courage, integrity, willingness, and humility to do this?

Our own sobriety is on the line: The overtures we're contemplating may be a snap, bringing us emotional catharsis and relief, or they may be quite difficult. How secure are we that we can handle any upset or disappointment? Usually by now we have plenty of sober references to remind us that we don't pick up no matter what. But this is a good time to tune up our spiritual condition and tighten our sober safety net—to increase the number of meetings we go to and check in with our sponsor more frequently.

That's why compiling our list of amends and becoming willing to make them is a Step in itself. We do Step Eight as if there is no Step Nine at all.

MAKING A LIST

Just as they told us not to rush out at Step Five and mumble apologies to all the exes we cheated on and employers we shortchanged, our sponsors may again tell us to slow down. We must be very thoughtful about whom we plan to approach and how and when we're going to do it. So for the moment, we're just making a list—that's it.

By now, we've learned that our recovery is about a lot more than just quitting meth. To treat our spiritual sickness, we have to change all kinds of attitudes and behaviors. When we did our inventory of fears and resentments, we considered our whole lives. Likewise, as we make our Step Eight list, we look at harm we caused not only when we were using, but also things we did before we ever picked up and after we stopped.

Many of us will be only too happy to hesitate: First, as addicts, we have a long history of being self-involved, so a great many of us will honestly believe that the only person we hurt, especially during our using, was ourselves. No doubt, we did injure ourselves, in body, mind, and spirit, and it's perfectly OK to note this in detail. But there were innocent bystanders nearby when we set our lives on fire. And some of them got burned.

The injuries we caused run the gamut—from violent crimes to thoughtlessness, absence, and neglect. (We cannot give an exhaustive list here; people hurt each other in millions of ways, some of them obvious, some of them deviously subtle.) Whether the harm we caused was grave or petty, we're often likely to minimize our transgressions. *Sure, I stole some money from my job, but it's such a big company no one even noticed.... Yes, I crashed a friend's car drunk years ago, but when I ran into them a few months ago, they made a joke about it—obviously they're not still upset.... I really did scream my head off a few times, but it's not like I hit him.... I knew it was a mistake to sleep with my best friend's girlfriend, but we were all so high that weekend....* That kind of thing. If we're not sure how much we really harmed someone, we put them down on the list to run by our sponsor. If we're rationalizing, they'll help us to see it.

Some of us have the opposite habit: We maximize our transgressions and play the martyr, making ourselves feel more important by overdramatizing some small slight. Our sponsors can help us see that, too. Having the objective perspective of a fellow we trust is enormously valuable. It's time to right-size our egos—and that will require all the humility we cultivated in Steps Six and Seven. Often our sponsors will build on the work from those Steps and ask us to describe the character defects we were acting on when we caused the harm under discussion. The more we understand why we behaved the way we did, the more willing we'll be to put that difficult name on our amends list.

When it comes to people we definitely know we hurt, our hesitations are different. Shame can be a powerful obstacle. It was hard enough at Step Five to tell our sponsor how we'd behaved; but it seems truly daunting to admit how awful we were *to the people we were awful to!* In most cases, they know what happened as well as we do. Acknowledging our shared history may be embarrassing, but ignoring a wound isn't the way to heal it. We have to stitch it up.

And then there are those people who don't even know we lied to them, stole from them, cheated on them. They're perfectly happy not knowing; do we really have to upset them—and more important, ourselves—with a terrible truth they probably don't want to hear? For now, we just put their names on our list. Whether or not we will make amends, and how we'll do it, are questions for another day.

For most of us, though, the hardest obstacle we'll have to overcome is our own resentment. After all, most of these people wronged us, too. All of us—every last one—will feel a sharp reluctance to approach certain people. *He's not a nice person.... She's too self-centered to even realize how much she hurt me.... What about the time he gave me an STI?...They were responsible for much more of the discord than I was!...* Yes, it's liberating to take responsibility for our actions—but who's supposed to take responsibility for *their* actions?

Their actions are their business, our sponsors tell us. We must try our best to forgive them and focus on what we did. We have no other choice. Their behavior is not "a thing we can change"—we're concerned only with the things we can. In short, we need to check our motives. In a lot of situations, setting our needs and desires aside won't be easy. As we contemplate each amends, we'll need to meditate and pray for the willingness to make things right even with people we bitterly resent. In the meantime, our sponsors can help us plan how and when to make our amends.

BECOMING WILLING

Sizing up the list, our sponsors may ask us, "Well, are you really willing to reach out to these people?" One great way to take the temperature of our willingness is to sort the names into three categories. First, who can we approach today? These are people who are still in our lives, people who may know we're in recovery and have encouraged us in our journey. Looking over this *now* list, we realize we're excited to see these folks and clear the air. We may even have made the amends we owed them already.

The next group of people we are willing to approach, but we're not able to do it just yet. Maybe we owe them some money and need to work out a payment plan. (If we've been bingeing on crystal for years, we may owe our landlords or families a lot of money!) Or they live in a different state—lots of us fled across country to escape our catastrophes—and we won't see them for some months. This *not yet* category will likely also include the names of a lot of folks we're still sore at, or who are still sore at us. We may need a bit more time to set aside our resentment. And they may need some time to see that we're really getting better before they'll entertain any overture. There's no huge obstacle to making these amends, but we'll need further meditation or prayer before we do them.

The main reason to wait to make an amends is that we want to be sure we aren't likely to repeat whatever it is we did. That's another sense of "amend"—to change. Have we changed? Is the work we did in Steps Six and Seven to alter our behavior sticking? Our sponsors would never encourage us to procrastinate in our Step work, but if we're still acting out in all sorts of rash ways, they may indeed tell us we need to slow down and finish working on ourselves before we approach the people from our past.

Finally, who do we believe we won't ever be able to approach? There may be people we really shouldn't engage, because it would be dangerous to them or us or do more harm; we'll speak more about that at Step Nine. But most of these *nevers* are of a different variety. Maybe we've injured someone who is no longer available to us. Perhaps we were alienated from a parent who's passed away, or a partner who told us in no uncertain terms they never want to see us again.

THE TWELVE STEPS

We may indeed be unable to ever approach these people. But there are others on our never list—usually people we cannot yet forgive—who we may someday be able to make amends to.

How many other things are we doing in recovery that we never thought would be possible? Doing the next right thing, we've changed in ways we once couldn't imagine. More is possible if we can only keep an open mind. For now, we don't need to dwell on what-may-be. As we said, we write out Step Eight as if there is no Step Nine. Today we are only making a list and working on becoming willing: We pray and meditate, we talk it out with our fellows, we humbly ask for help removing our shortcomings, and we show up for life sober. Day by day, our willingness grows.

FORGIVENESS

In most cases, doing the inventory in Four and Five and letting go of our character defects in Six and Seven have cultivated some humility in us, and the willingness to set things right. If we aren't quite sure how willing we are to approach this or that person, there's an easy way to figure it out. We ask ourselves, Have I forgiven them? After all, we're about to ask them to forgive us.

It won't be easy, but we must ask for the willingness to forgive all of them. Mind you, most of the time they won't have made any approach to us; they may not even know we believe they've wronged us. We have to accept that they may never apologize to us or try to make us whole. Can we find the understanding to set aside our harsh judgments and forgive them anyway? Usually, the answer is yes, but sometimes, it's an emphatic no! And that's OK. If we can't quite forgive someone, can we nonetheless put down our grudge? Are we ready to make our amends without any expectation of an apology from them? Often, we'll be astonished by what

STEP EIGHT

happens in a messy relationship when we clean up our part.

The principle most often associated with Step Eight is love. We're cultivating true compassion for others: Having examined our own conduct and charted our resentments and fears, we've gained solid insights into how the human ego can be wounded. The great gift of Steps Four, Five, Six, and Seven is empathy—we've learned how fragile we are, and that naturally unlocks some sympathy for everyone around us. They have many of the same blocked, faulty instincts we do! At this stage of the Steps, many of us find we have nothing but love for the people in our life. Maybe especially the people who've harmed us, or whom we have harmed.

We will need a lot of love indeed to proceed to Step Nine. Soon, we'll take everything we've learned so far out on the road and formally reach out to the people we've harmed, possibly for the first time. Now we're not only willing to make those amends—we're also mindful about why we're doing it, and confident that we're prepared for whatever outcome may arise.

STEP

Made direct amends to such people wherever possible, except when to do so would injure them or others.

STEP NINE

We've come a long way in our recovery. By the time we get to Step Nine, we have dispelled our denial. We know how we behaved and who was affected; more and more, we see the flaws in our old approach to the world and are starting to understand how it no longer serves us; and day by day we're humbly modeling a new way to act in almost every situation. Even more astonishing, we've been able to forgive most of the people we believe wronged us, or to at least set aside our grudges. Our experience so far proves that our most hardened assumptions can change.

Films about people working Twelve Step programs always feature a Step Nine reconciliation scene. The drama in such encounters is irresistible. Usually it goes like this: The recovering addict offers a check to pay for the wrecked car or the smashed greenhouse or the stolen jewelry, but Mom or Dad or the kindly boss refuses the money. Bursting into tears, the addict insists. *"You don't understand. I have to do this for me!"* Making our amends may not be remotely cinematic or all that emotional, but even when they're anticlimactic, they're essential to our progress as sober human beings. We need to let go of that incapacitating feeling of remorse, repair our damaged spirits, and gain the freedom to face every corner of our world.

And the movies are only half-right, anyway. Yes, we have to do this work for us, but it's just as important for the people we've wronged. By this stage of our journey, we're learning to put others' needs first. In our amends, we focus on the people we've harmed, and how we can try to make them whole. When we approach people, we try not to think about things they may have done to us at all. We concentrate on how we've wronged them and how they need mending, or the exercise won't benefit anyone, least of all ourselves.

We may or may not experience the profound emotional or spiritual growth our fellows say they felt doing this Step.

THE TWELVE STEPS

That's ultimately not the point. We make amends because it's simply the right thing to do.

DIRECT AMENDS

Perhaps that's why the Step tells us we are making "direct amends," not apologizing. Certainly, our overtures will usually include an apology, but we must also offer to repair any damage we caused.

Whenever possible, we make an amends face-to-face. We don't just intrude on someone's day out of nowhere and drop a bomb; we have to make sure they're willing to see us and give us some of their time. And when we do meet, we come prepared: If we took money from our ex-boss, we have it with us when we meet, or at least the first payment. If we kicked in Mom's television, we offer to replace it. What we need to do is usually pretty obvious. But even then, we're careful to follow our sponsor's guidance. They can—and will—recommend good, specific ways to make an amends that takes into account our whole situation.

Apologizing for what happened is only the beginning. A broad "I'm sorry" is only so useful. Most of us have spent our lives spewing out empty excuses; we know how hollow words can be. And an apology is all too easy to qualify: "I'm so sorry *for that time we were fighting* and I called you all those nasty names. I promise that will never happen again." Instead of describing events, we focus on behaviors: "I'm so sorry I lash out at you and call you nasty things. I'm learning to do better." In Steps Six and Seven, we saw that our poor choices weren't isolated aberrations but the unavoidable products of our warped coping mechanisms. And in Step Eight, getting clear about our motives was one way we became willing to make our amends. In Step Nine, we aren't rationalizing our past behavior, we are mending the damage whatever we did caused. That we're able to do so is the best evidence we have of how profoundly we've changed.

Most of the time, the people we're reaching out to for these clear-cut amends know what was going on with us. Nonetheless, we don't hide behind our addiction to minimize our behavior. If they bring it up, then of course we can talk about what happened and the changes we are making. Our sponsors tell us this is not the time for righteousness or dramatic self-flagellation. In fact, once we've said our piece, we should ask if we've left anything out. Memories differ, and we never really know the depths of another's heart. We must let the person we've wounded express their feelings on their own terms. If they're carrying around a painful burden, we have an opportunity to help them put it down. To keep us focused on the task at hand, some of our sponsors offer a bit of coaching, even giving us a simple script to follow.

Yes, technology is continually advancing, but there will likely always be amends we can't make face-to-face for some reason or other. That's OK—they can be just as meaningful in other forms, too. Sometimes, circumstances dictate a long-distance communication. If someone is across an ocean, we may need to write them a letter. (A letter is almost always better than a phone call in such cases: Putting something in writing forces us to be clear and thorough and requires a bit more accountability.) If someone refuses to communicate with us at all, we must respect that, but we might instead volunteer for a charity that aligns with their worldview. And if someone has died, we will need to find some other way to repair any damage. Rituals, prayer, and meditation can be lovely, but we can honor a lost friend or parent even more concretely by taking part in activities they relished, and giving back to people they loved.

So far, we're still in the *now* section of our Step Eight list. Things get a bit tricky when we get to the *not yets*. It may be a logistical matter—not having the money to repay a friend, or not being able to travel to see our parents in person. But this category will likely also include people we've hurt deeply who aren't ready to entertain even our most heartfelt apologies. We've had the benefit of working Steps Four through Seven, so we know we aren't likely to repeat the same behavior today—but they may not be so sure. This is the main reason our sponsors told us to wait until we had a bit of sobriety before making our amends. We need some time to become open-minded, willing, and humble; the people in our lives may need even more to see how we've changed.

LIVING AMENDS

For these *not yets,* we get to work anyway, by making what's called a living amends. If our boss is fed up with our excuses, we stop offering them, and instead show up on time with a good attitude and work our butt off. If we've disappointed our families, we demonstrate through consistent actions that we've changed, returning our parents' calls promptly and not picking fights about religion or politics with Grandma. If our partner is so wounded that they barely speak to us, we commit to carrying our weight at home and living up to our commitments. Down the road, once we've earned their trust again, we can make a formal apology and offer the specific reparation they need.

We also make living amends when we've lost touch with the people we've harmed. If we were a shoddy housepainter or a rude waiter or an inattentive teacher, we take pains to perform our jobs with care and treat everyone with dignity. If we kept our whole building up at all hours and constantly left a mess in the recycling room, we go out of our way to be quiet, respectful, and neat neighbors. If we were sexually compulsive, we may well have passed on STIs to countless strangers. In recovery, honesty is a cornerstone of our sexual ideal; we take care of ourselves, and take care to take care of others, too. We have a karmic debt to repay: We're glad now to be a worker among workers, a neighbor among neighbors, a lover among lovers.

If we became dealers in active addiction, or coaxed people in our circle to try new drugs or take other risks, we can make one obvious living amends—not to sell crystal meth or other drugs. We might also make ourselves available to help former contacts find recovery if they need it. This doesn't mean we become sober preachers, but we don't shy from sharing with others who ask exactly why and how we're getting better. Some of us may have committed even more serious crimes. There might be no way to make a direct amends to someone we've gravely injured, but there are many ways to make restitution to society at large. And if we're doing our living amends by living behind bars, we strive to serve our time with humility and grace.

All of this may sound like a tall order, but if we were thorough in Steps Six and Seven, we're already making living amends. We are trying today not to react to conflicts out of instinct and instead take more thoughtful actions in all kinds of situations. The ingenious structure of the program reveals itself again: Each successive Step builds on the one before.

WHEREVER POSSIBLE

Many of the Steps contain careful caveats to make the work more forgiving for us: We *come* to believe; we *make a decision* to turn our will over; we *become willing* to let go of defects. At Nine, the caveat is extensive, but it isn't there primarily for our benefit: We make direct amends "to such people wherever possible, except when to do so would injure them or others."

There are many situations where making a direct amends is impossible because we'd further wound the very people we want to heal. If we've been mean about someone behind their back, sharing every last scrap of gossip with them would be cruel. If we've been unfaithful to our partner, an itemized schedule of infidelities might cripple their self-esteem. We've been carrying around a heavy burden, but no matter how desperately we want to put it down, getting whatever it is off our chest isn't always the right thing to do.

We can't get spiritual relief when we cause somebody else pain. Using, we didn't care who we hurt; now that we're sober, we go out of our way to do no harm. This doesn't mean we're off the hook—quite the contrary. It's simply kinder in many cases to offer an oblique apology. When we can't be specific, we redouble our efforts to make a complete living amends.

Let us be clear: We should never attempt Step Nine on our own. We need our sponsor or some other spiritual guide to help us weigh the unintended consequences of our overtures. Consider the situation of a third party in an extramarital affair. They were already the victim of our advances; they shouldn't now be the victim of our righteousness. We ought to also think about the well-being of our family. As much as we may feel the need to come clean to our workplace about our negligence or petty thieving—or to the authorities, for crimes that went unpunished—we have to ask: How will we feed our children if we get fired or locked up? When these situations arise, our sponsors will have useful guidance.

LETTING GO OF THE RESULTS

By and large, people are very forgiving when we make our amends. Because we don't usually make them until we've been sober for a while—a year or more, for most of us—there's plenty of evidence that we have sincerely changed from the destructive, selfish people we became in our

STEP NINE

addiction. In many cases, the amends will be a springboard for renewed intimacy.

But occasionally, even a direct and straightforward Ninth Step amends will go poorly. We can never know for certain how we will be received; sometimes, the other person has no interest in our apology or restitution. They're not willing to forgive us—they may not want to listen to us at all. All we can do is turn it over, trusting we made our best effort. We must respect their boundaries until the day comes, if it comes, when they're ready to accept our contrition.

Our sponsors prepare us for this possibility—all along the program has been teaching us we cannot control every interaction—but they tell us we have to make the amends whatever happens. We're learning "to take the action and let go of the results." This is what it means to be responsible: to truly respect other people, to forgive them without reservations, to love them without expectations.

Anyway, if an amends isn't received well, that doesn't mean it's somehow "bad." If we've demonstrated our willingness to set matters straight, then we have succeeded. We've done our job and tried to make something right. Often our sponsors encourage us to take a moment alone for prayer and meditation after we approach someone. We may want to express new gratitude. Or we might need to ask for the serenity to accept something we cannot change.

When we hesitate—and all of us will hesitate!—our fellows may ask us, "How free do you want to be?" Making amends is the best tool we have to achieve peace of mind. If we really want to free ourselves from the resentments and fears of our past, and clear today's hesitations from the horizon, we will put it to use.

LIFE ON LIFE'S TERMS

It's liberating to reach this point in the Steps. To the best of

THE TWELVE STEPS

our ability, we have cleared away the messes of our past. As new conflicts arise, we stay attuned to our habitual patterns and take contrary actions instead. When we do screw up, we have a handy way to dispatch our resentments and calm our fears. In all matters, we're well-practiced at doing the next right thing and letting go of the results. Finally, we've found the humility, willingness, and love to approach people we've wronged and try to repair the damage.

Almost all of us found we need to make an amends to ourselves. And day by day, staying sober and "living life on life's terms," we are. If we put our own names at the bottom of our Step Eight list—and many of us do—our sponsors will ask us to be concrete in our restitution. Of course, we began to treat ourselves better the moment we put down crystal meth; and by Steps Six and Seven, we've learned to practice self-care. Some sponsors suggest specific things we can do for our physical, emotional, and spiritual well-being, to pay off the deficit of disregard we built up over the years. Others say that the only way we can totally make amends to ourselves is to finish approaching everyone else on our list. If we've made things right with all the people in our lives, that crippling feeling of remorse will finally begin to lift. Our spirits will feel light, and we'll have a new optimism.

By now, you may have heard the Ninth Step Promises, from the Big Book, read at our meetings. The Promises talk about our growing self-esteem and assurance in the world, but mostly they describe freedom. Having come through the inventory and amends process, we can trust ourselves again: "We will intuitively know how to handle situations which used to baffle us." Think of how miraculous that is.

We used to make every problem worse, but now we can rely again on our intuition in most situations. We know better, we do better—we are better. It's an achievement worth

STEP NINE

celebrating: Not only are we remaining free from active addiction, but we're also at long last behaving like full-fledged adults. Day by day, we'll have a bit more ease handling whatever the next challenge might be. The remaining Steps offer still more help with that lifelong project.

STEP

10

Continued to take personal inventory and when we were wrong promptly admitted it.

STEP TEN

With the last three Steps, we've reached what many of us call the maintenance phase of our recovery. To continue moving forward, we'll have to stay actively engaged. To keep growing spiritually, we need to practice what we've learned and try to live with balance and discipline. Our spirituality is like a bicycle: Periodically, we have to tighten the brakes, oil the chain, and scrub away any mud and rust. Whether we've been sober two weeks or two decades, we only get a daily reprieve from the disease of addiction. So when we say we do periodic spiritual maintenance, we mean we try to do it every day.

But you knew that. By now, you've seen that living sober doesn't result in perpetual ecstasy. Sometimes the world will seem like a Day-Glo disco playing all your favorite songs, but more often than not there will be dull days. And all of us will face difficulties. Getting clean doesn't mean we're no longer human beings. The difference now is we try not to carry our agony around, festering over mistakes or perceived slights. Today we can pause, take a breath, and clear our head; we can pray and meditate; we can reach out and connect with our friends and fellows.

And when it's time to act, we've got tools available to help us solve whatever problem is troubling us. Working with our sponsors, we've learned a straightforward way to respond to any emotional upset. We've used the inventory and amends process to work through our past resentments and continuing fears: looking for our part in conflicts, slowly letting go of our unfounded anxieties and character defects, and forgiving others and cleaning up the messes we made. Step Ten is the pocket guide to that whole system, helping us to make things right promptly, the moment we recognize we're in trouble.

PROMPTLY

Of course, "promptly" is a word subject to many interpretations. (In the fossil record, for example, mammals promptly succeed the dinosaurs.) How swiftly we recognize a problem, acknowledge our part, and make amends will vary from situation to situation. But if we've done Steps One through Nine, we no longer have to mindlessly behave like a jerk or wallow in perpetual self-pity. We try to take action the minute a problem is apparent. The Latin root of promptly, *promptus*, means "visible." If we can see it, we do something about it.

And we don't generally need any prompting to get to work. Our sponsors have patiently guided us through the first nine Steps. At Ten, we take the training wheels off the bike. We're intimately acquainted with our historical resentments, persistent fears, and habitual character defenses. We know our modus operandi, and we're devoted to changing it day by day. But though we ought to be able to pedal that bike through our difficulties without getting a push, we do need one sometimes. In the first place, we can act promptly on something only if we're aware of it. And we can't always see our side of the street without a bit of perspective. As we said discussing Steps Six and Seven, our instincts are deeply ingrained. Old-timers in the fellowship like to say we "move at the speed of pain." The program has been designed to help us recognize and accept our pain and then transcend it. Do we want to feel better? We just have to be willing to try.

So we reach out for help. A lot of the time, our chats with our sponsors and other fellows may not seem to be about staying clean at all—instead, they're dedicated to "I can't believe she said that to me," or "I'm certainly not picking up the phone!" or "I just don't know the next move to make." Our friends listen, offer their observations, and ask pointed questions about our resentments and fears—but

STEP TEN

generally they reach a point in the conversation when they say, "Maybe you ought to write this out…?"

SPOT INVENTORY

Once it's clear something is upsetting us, there's no good reason to postpone our treatment. The cure isn't onerous— we just have to write it out, identify our part in the problem, and then take whatever action is needed. Our sponsors can suggest many specific ways to do this. A lot of our fellows recommend using the five-column table we described at Step Four.

Say we're having an issue with our boss. We might write:

WHO *Who hurt me?*	HOW *What did they do to harm me?*	WHERE *What instinct was hurt?*	MY PART *What role did I play? How do I nurse this grudge?*	CHARACTER DEFECTS *How did I act out? What was I afraid of?*
My boss	She changed my schedule without any warning; now my weekend plans are wrecked. She's incompetent and totally demanding.	Touches my security and interferes with my intimate relationships. I was on my way out of town with my partner.	My expectations are out of whack. I knew when I took the job that our schedules could change with short notice. I don't know how hard it is for her to juggle all of our shifts. My ego really needs to be right-sized.	*Anger:* I sent her a sharp email complaining. If I'd been agreeable, she'd have at least let me get out an hour early to make the train. *Character assassination:* I ran her down to my two work pals. *Pride:* How dare she ask me to do the thing she hired me to do! *Fear of being ignored* *Fear of not having enough*

The answers we need are always right in front of us. Once again, we see the danger of unreasonable expectations. We're reminded that we have to practice acceptance in our dealings with others. Our thinking proceeds as follows: I have to forgive her—if she's sometimes scattershot with the scheduling, it's not all her fault; it's hard to juggle a dozen

THE TWELVE STEPS

people's needs. I should do a living amends—the next time someone complains about her, I won't pile on; I'll say something nice about her instead. And I have to make a real amends for my nasty email. I'll write a simple apology for being cranky, and run it by my sponsor real quick before I send it.

There are great advantages to this approach, doing a brief Fourth and Fifth Step over a specific fear or resentment. It keeps our focus squarely on the one variable of the equation we can solve: ourselves. We'll get better, even if the relationship in question remains fraught. We tune in at once to the instincts at work and concentrate on taking contrary actions (Six and Seven), to help us handle these new challenges. And we make a prompt amends (Eight and Nine) as needed to defuse any conflict before it becomes a war.

As simple as this sounds, it doesn't come easily. Remember—we have running-away disease: We're terrified of stopping where we are, facing our misgivings, owning our mistakes, and making things right. Being willing to apologize is a trait everyone admires: colleagues, friends, family, lovers. Working Step Ten helps us foster honest connections in all our relationships. When we use it to address a strictly personal problem—our fear of intimacy, perhaps, or our tendency to procrastinate—it can be a great aid to deepen self-knowledge, leading us to profound spiritual growth.

But our need for this Step is even more basic than that. Step Ten helps us stay sane. Addicts are by nature restless souls. When we're disturbed about something, we have a tendency to fester over it. It could be a work problem like the one described above; an argument with our parents, or worse, our children; a romantic or sexual misadventure; or a million other kinds of conflicts and frustrations. Our irritability about the situation spreads to other areas of our life, and soon we're unhappy with everyone we know and even total strangers, yelling at waiters and store clerks. We're prone to magnify our difficulties out of all proportion; our minor annoyances quickly metastasize into all-encompassing discontentment. And our history tells us where that can lead: back to drugs.

That's why this Step is critical. We cannot be present if we're stuck in our fears and resentments. And we won't stay sober if we can't be present. So we put our pen to paper. (Or even the back of an envelope or a napkin if it's urgent!) Doing Step Ten clears out our spirit, making us available for whatever surprise today holds.

SPIRITUAL CHECK-INS

Thankfully, most days we do not find ourselves in any kind of crisis. Our sponsors told us way back in the beginning that we'd have an easier time getting out of our hole if we'd put down our shovel and stop digging. In recovery, we're no longer running from failure to failure; more often, we stroll from success to success. To keep ourselves walking through the world with calm and dedication, we lean on a variety of healthy habits. We keep going to meetings regularly and stay in touch with our sponsor. We start our days with a simple surrender, praying or meditating or jotting down a gratitude list. We show up for ourselves and the people in our lives, saying yes to challenges we once would have bolted from.

Doing a regular Tenth Step, even when things seem to be fine, is another terrific tool. It offers us a chance to see not only how we're acting on our character defects, but also how we're drawing on our assets. Many of us build on the practice we learned at Step Six of taking a quiet moment when we climb into bed to look back at our day. This kind of meditation can also form the foundation for our Eleventh Step. We ask ourselves how we're feeling, yes, but more important, we ask what we're doing. How did I do today?

THE TWELVE STEPS

Did I stay sober?
Did I connect with people?
Did I run on my willpower, or was I able to
    surrender control?
Did I react to people or situations out of resentment
    or fear?
Did I hold myself accountable to anyone?
Did I remember to be gentle on myself when I fell
    into old habits?
Did I do something that was hard for me?
Did I forgive anyone?
Did I apologize to anyone and clean up any messes?
Did I show up for myself and take care of my business?
Did I stay in touch with my Higher Power?
Did I help anyone?

These questions roughly track the Twelve Steps, but there is no set list. Your check-in might run longer or shorter. To get into the habit, we might write out our answers for a month or two. Where we uncover resentments or fears, we can call our sponsor. They'll encourage us to proceed to an inventory, and we'll do it (yes, promptly). Eventually, most of us learn to do these spot inventories on our own, and tell our sponsor about it after.

We've worked very hard to stay sober. And we're committed to keep on working. Our new life requires discipline and perseverance—those are the principles commonly associated with Step Ten. If the program ever seems too rigorous and difficult, we remind ourselves that it's all practice. Everything we do is practice! In fact, lots of things that used to seem hard are becoming easier. We may not even recognize ourselves today. Once, we couldn't show up and couldn't be trusted. Now we're dependable, and our word is good. We do what we say, and we say what we mean. We have integrity.

STEP TEN

STEP

*Sought through prayer
and meditation to improve
our conscious contact with
a God of our understanding
praying only for the
knowledge of God's will
for us, and the power
to carry that out.*

STEP ELEVEN

Scientists say the universe tends toward disorder. Well, human beings aren't any different. We need to keep moving toward something, or we'll eventually fall apart. Step Ten, frequently taking stock of how we're doing in our relationships and with our responsibilities, helps us stay conscious in our recovery. Further developing this consciousness is at the core of Eleven. If Ten helps us keep our spiritual bicycle tuned up—so we can continue pedaling along toward our destination—Eleven is there because, eventually, we're going to get a flat tire. If we're in touch with our Higher Power and trust we're on the right path, we won't unravel when things go wrong.

The "prayer and meditation" Step reiterates what we learned in Steps Two and Three, that our Higher Power is our own business—but whatever it is, we should reach out toward it. Our contact with the God of our understanding must be "conscious." We must listen to the universe and try to decipher our purpose in it.

Those of us who practice a religion will be more familiar with this idea of staying in contact with a Higher Power, though recovery may be teaching us to do it for new reasons and possibly in new ways. Agnostics may wonder if whatever force there is in the universe can communicate with us at all—or would even want to. And atheists will likely scoff at the whole notion, at least at first: How do you have a conversation with something that has no awareness? Some of us just set aside the whole question. Instead of praying to a Higher Power for guidance, we reach down to a Deeper Power—the life force, or "unsuspected inner resource" that lies beneath our consciousness.

These are all great questions, and we have the rest of our lives to ponder them. But metaphysical considerations are not what brought us into the program. We aren't reinventing spirituality; we just believe that for us in recovery, we need to seek out conscious contact with the God of our understanding. Whether *it* is in contact with *us* depends on our conception of our Higher Power. The ultimate answer to the God question is that there is no answer. Our thoughts on spiritual matters will continue to evolve: Note the wording of the Step: It's not "Prayed and meditated to improve…" but *"Sought* through prayer and meditation to improve…" Step Eleven doesn't tell us we have to find anything concrete—it only asks us to keep seeking.

We don't need certainty on this topic to see that we do better when we're more mindful. Practicing mindfulness is a good idea for everyone, by the way, not just addicts. But those of us who went through the hell of using know what it means to live *un*consciously: Bumping along from reaction to reaction, giving in to every selfish impulse regardless of the consequences, we ended up spiritually disconnected from everyone and everything. And that isolation almost killed us. Staying in contact with God or the universe or whatever we want to call it, we never need to be alone again.

PRAYER

It's said that praying is asking God a question, and meditating is listening for the answer. Our faith tradition or personal philosophy may dispose us to do more of one or the other. Some of us, being religious, pray habitually and fervently; others who are more secular find peace in regular meditation. But Step Eleven is unambiguous: It says we should pray *and* meditate. No matter what spiritual practice we follow, we ask for guidance and listen for answers.

We've described the practice of prayer throughout this guide. We hope that, like us, you have found prayers that help calm your soul and center your intentions. Or written your own prayers, as many of us do. You'll notice the prayers we use have one thing in common—they don't really ask for anything specific. In recovery, we don't rely on the wishing prayers of our childhood ("God, please tell Santa to bring me Malibu Barbie") or the foxhole prayers of active addiction ("If you get me through this urine test, I will never get high again"). Instead, we ask only for calm acceptance, the willingness to grow, the courage to change. We ask to be teachable. Our crystal meth careers taught us that doing things our way only leads to catastrophe. We went to war with reality, hiding instead in a shrinking, false fantasy. The Steps align us with the world as it is; our prayers nudge us to join that world and find our purpose within it.

Our relationship with our Higher Power is always growing; the way we talk with God will likely change as well over the course of our recovery. Most of us try to communicate with our H.P. daily; it becomes a natural part of our morning routine, or follows naturally from our nightly Tenth Step check-ins. As with everything we do, there are no rules. How we reach out—and how we listen—is a very personal matter. As the conversation proceeds day by day, we heighten our intuition and become more comfortable in our skin and the world.

MEDITATION

For a lot of us, Step Eleven is our first encounter with meditation. The practice dates back at least 4,000 years, to early Hinduism, and it's featured prominently in most religious traditions since. It grows out of our desire for quiet reflection, which may be the essence of human consciousness. Other creatures seem to do this, too—you've seen a cat sitting in a sunny spot, staring into the distance. What is he doing? He's listening, watching, breathing. He's in the moment.

This sort of passive meditation, with an animal, is a great place to start. If you have a dog, try leaving your phone at home when you walk, and just follow her wherever she goes. Or if you like to garden, the next time you're out there digging, just focus your mind on the plants in your care. Exercising is a good time to experiment, too. We get some of our best ideas when we're biking, jogging, walking, doing yoga. Putting on our makeup, taking a shower, making music or art—even housework can be intensely spiritual. Doing the dishes is a great time to check in with the universe. The key is to listen to whatever may come.

Practicing mindfulness like this, we learn to be present in our body, mind, and breath, to what's happening inside us as well as our surroundings. To turn on this inner life, a lot of us find it helps to turn everything else off—our TVs, our computers, and especially our phones. We surround ourselves with noise and distraction because it can be terrifying to experience silence, to be alone with the cacophony of our own inner monologue. Allowing ourselves to hear our own thoughts can reveal so much. A lot of that noise is just the voice of our ego; we're so used to it, we can't hear anything else.

We ought to pause here and recognize how far we've come. We were speedfreaks, and now we are consciously trying to slow down. We worshipped at the altar of more—more drugs, more dancing, more screwing, more fidgeting, and oh so much more chatting—and now we want less. Silence and stillness were anathema to us, and here we are, seeking them out. It doesn't matter how long we've been sober; it will never be easy to turn down the volume on Radio Me.

A more formal practice of meditation will take us beyond mindfulness to an even deeper, more mysterious place: inside ourselves. To do this, a lot of us seek out help. We ask our sponsors and other fellows for guidance. Many of them encourage us to try something more active, a guided meditation. Sitting in a chair in a circle, we strive to be present for whatever thoughts arise, without judging or holding on to them. We focus on our breath, which only happens in the moment—if we're listening to our body and know where we are, we're already practicing mindfulness. We can take this further and use a mantra: With each inhale, we might breathe in faith; with each exhale, we might breathe out fear. Remember what we said about respiration and the spirit? Our lungs may be our most spiritual organ. In that silence between breaths, what do we hear? What do we begin to see? What do we know?

We start small and keep it simple. If we can sit quietly for even 45 seconds, that's huge. As straightforward as this sounds, it can be truly scary at first. What if I can't sit still? What if I can't clear my mind? What is waiting for me in that silence? We don't overcome these anxieties so much as we learn to live with them. People who meditate describe it as the simple act of trying to meditate. So we keep on trying!

Eventually, we may attempt to meditate on our own at home. We don't need a Zen garden and bells and incense. A comfortable chair will do. We close our eyes and breathe in…and out…and in…and out…. Once this becomes easier, some of us try other variations. Our sponsors, always eager for us to read and write, might recommend doing a 5-5-5: Five minutes of reading, five minutes of meditation, and five minutes of writing. Soon we can graduate to a 10-10-10, or even a 15-15-15.

We may not believe it at first, but even the hardest-core tweaker can slow down their racing stream of consciousness. It may take a while—some say it was years before they could quiet the noise in their heads. But all of us have the capacity to be still. What comes to us in those quiet moments? What do we find in this second, in the now? That's between us and our Higher Power.

AWARENESS

There's no right way to pray or meditate. How could there be? There are as many approaches to spirituality as there are

THE TWELVE STEPS

people on Earth. The suggestions we offer here are merely that, possible paths we might take among the endless number the universe offers. Seeking out one may lead to another and another and another...

Step Eleven simply and beautifully invites us to keep searching. We are breathing into this moment, developing a sense of curiosity and kindness toward ourselves, and becoming more open to the universe around us. We ask for guidance and listen for direction—for "knowledge of God's will for us, and the power to carry that out." Different as they are, our spiritual practices all share this focus: How can I be most useful? What does the universe want me to do? What's my job today?

Our journey from selfishness and denial to selflessness and awareness is never finished. Prayer and meditation give us a personal map to this new universe.

STEP ELEVEN

STEP

Having had a spiritual awakening as a result of these steps, we tried to carry this message to crystal meth addicts, and to practice these principles in all of our affairs.

What do we mean by a spiritual awakening? Put simply, we have changed. Each of us would describe it differently. Are we becoming free from the compulsion to use crystal meth? Do we communicate with a Higher Power of our own understanding? Are we able to accept the things we cannot change and courageously get to work on the things we can? Have we learned to set aside our toxic resentments, and do we often succeed at checking self-sabotaging impulses? Are we quicker to pay debts and ready to apologize when we screw up? Are we less prone to self-obsession, do we find ourselves thinking of others more often? Are we eager to give back to a world we thought had left us for dead? Yes.

We've learned a system for living that helps us handle the difficulties that used to trip us up. We are accepting ourselves and connect with others. We have the integrity to show up for our jobs and the courage to take risks on new careers. We have a healthy approach to our love and sex lives. Where once we ran away from the world, now we calmly walk toward it. In active addiction, our spirits slept; doing the Steps has woken them up.

Some of us may have had a religious experience or some other sort of "white light" moment, but for most, the epiphany dawned gently over time. Suddenly or slowly, something profound has shifted in our spirit, or our personality, our thinking—again, each of us would probably use a different word—and now the impossible seems possible.

The way we used to live may seem foreign to us now. Every day back then brought a new frenzy but the same old insanity. We could never get enough of anything when we were using crystal meth. But taking more, more, more, always more left us with nothing. In recovery, we search for less—less drama, less chaos, less ego—and find everything. Our ever-smaller prison cell has become an ever-expanding universe of possibilities.

THE TWELVE STEPS

Some days are better than others, sure. We're human beings, prone to thwarted expectations and all sorts of other frustrations. We'll probably never be paragons of virtue—that's not what the program asks of us. Indeed, the moment we claim perfection, we're lost. But we must never give up on progress. Day by day, we have the chance to move closer to our ideals.

Step Twelve doesn't represent some kind of graduation. The spiritual awakening it describes simply sums up what's already happened to us in Steps One through Eleven: "Having had a spiritual awakening…" Long before we got to Twelve, if we've stayed clean and done the work, we've come back to life. Something sublime has happened along the way.

But now, as always, we have more work to do. This Step has two distinct parts—and they can both seem pretty enormous: trying to carry the message of recovery to other crystal meth addicts; and practicing these principles in all of our affairs.

CARRYING THE MESSAGE IN THE ROOMS

Someone was there to shake our hand or offer us a hug when we walked into our first CMA meeting. Someone was there to tell her story, giving us our first chance to identify with a fellow addict. People were there to keep the meeting running in the first place. Later, someone was willing to sponsor us. Fellows have shared in our journey at every step. All of them were carrying the message.

And we've been passing it on, too, whether we knew it or not. The moment we first showed up to a meeting, we began showing up for each other. Nervous and confused as we were, we modeled willingness and surrender for the rest of the group. Day by day, we quietly helped each other by offering a friendly ear and sharing honestly. Our fellows identified with us as we described our challenges and triumphs—and we identified with them. Simply knowing we weren't alone pulled us further along toward recovery. The Steps begin with we: "We admitted we were powerless…" Not I. We cannot get sober alone; our recovery is something we build together.

In other words, most of us are working this Step before we even get to it. Many of us found ourselves doing various jobs while we were still counting days. "Service keeps us sober," our sponsors told us, encouraging us to help out by setting up chairs, making coffee, handing out sobriety chips, and so on. The group was there when we needed it, welcoming and safe—of course we were eager to do our part to keep it running smoothly.

In time, we were asked to speak at a meeting; or we got nominated to be a group's secretary or treasurer. Our sponsors told us to always say yes to service, and where recovery is concerned, we generally did as we were told. Perhaps our interest and talent led us to get involved at the intergroup: We took a shift each week answering the helpline, or, remembering the people who brought us meetings in jail or rehab, we volunteered to do the same. CMA is a large fellowship, we discovered, that needed a wide variety of talents and a diverse array of voices to keep functioning. Chipping in to help it operate, we made an important investment in our own recovery.

There were times we held back. Maybe we were still prone to procrastination, or paralyzed by a fear of failure. Or we still struggled with low self-esteem that talked us out of trying new things, accepting new challenges. The stakes seemed too high—people were counting on us to help them stay sober!—so we decided it was better to let some other fellow take on the job. Our sponsors gently reminded us that nobody in CMA is an expert. Strictly speaking, the only thing that was ever asked of us was to share our own experience, strength, and hope. If we had practice staying sober using the Steps, we had exactly what we needed to help another addict.

Isn't that what attracted us to the program? Here were people just as sick as we were who were getting better, a day at a time. Part of getting better, it turns out, is carrying the message. So we say yes to service. Our sponsors call this doing an esteemable act; over time, contributing to the fellowship even in small ways, we can build the self-esteem we've been missing. Giving back what's been given to us isn't just good karma. It's the best way we know to nurture our own recovery.

SPONSORSHIP

Crystal Meth Anonymous is a Twelve Step program, so the central pillar of service we do is leading others through the Steps. It's a privilege to be asked, and a joy to do. There's nothing as exciting as seeing someone come back to life using the tools of the program.

The prospect terrified us at first. Thinking back on the patient support and love we got from our sponsors, we were sure we couldn't ever be so open and generous. But our anxiety was misplaced. Our sponsors were once just as scared as we were; when they were unsure about how to handle a situation, all they did was ask their sponsors. And that's all we had to do.

An anxious first-time sponsor once called his sponsor in a fit. His sponsee had slipped again, and he wasn't sure he was helping. "Did you pick up today?" his sponsor asked. "Well, no," he answered. The reply: "Sounds like you're doing your job!" We are not parents, or psychiatrists, or financial advisers, or best friends—each of us is just one addict patiently sharing with another how we stay sober. If we're staying clean a day at a time, we have all the experience we need to help.

Sponsoring takes us back to Step One, because we are truly powerless over our sponsees. Sometimes they dive into recovery, sometimes they don't. Sometimes, we'll realize we're not the best fit for someone. Maybe they need more structure or more leeway than we're comfortable with. That's totally fine! When this happens, we don't "fire" the sponsee—they haven't been working for us!—we help them find someone more in sync with their needs. And long after they've moved on, we're always available to listen, offer suggestions, or give a friendly hug.

In time, every sponsor figures out this truth: We get just as much from the relationship as our sponsees do. "We have to give it away in order to keep it," the saying goes. In a practical, day-to-day manner, nothing is better at keeping us right-sized than turning off our own self-centered soundtrack and picking up the phone to listen to somebody else's troubles. And the actual work we do—helping a fellow through the Steps—keeps us grounded in our own program. We can't carry a message we aren't living ourselves. Answering questions, explaining concepts, and gently guiding someone through the process, we quietly take the journey again with them. We get to see the program through someone else's eyes. Working with others, we're perpetually learning, reinvesting in our recovery, and deepening our relationship with our fellows and our Higher Power.

SAYING YES TO SERVICE

Like we said, Step Twelve is not the epilogue to the program; it's an essential instruction to anyone who wants to stay sober and nurture their recovery. Whether sponsoring others, doing other kinds of program service, or contributing in our lives outside the fellowship, our attitude is simple: If something needs doing, we do it. We not only want to get whatever it is done, we also know that doing the work will help us stay clean.

Occasionally, though, we do say no to service. But what we're really saying is "not right now." If our enthusiasm has gotten the better of us, and we're stretched too thin, we won't have much to offer when we're needed. We're also careful, as in everything, to check our motives. While program work helps to keep us sober, we take care not to use it as an excuse to avoid obligations at our job or home. Sometimes, we'll be tempted to work with a newcomer for the wrong reasons. Maybe we're attracted to them, or they're in a position to help our career. If from the outset our aim in a relationship seems murky, it may be best to step aside. Nothing should come between us and our primary purpose, to carry the message.

One common obstacle we're likely to face doing service is our ego. It feels good to do an esteemable act for the group or the fellowship as a whole—we do this "for fun, and for free," as one old-timer likes to say—but we can get wrapped up in it. We love to feel indispensable, but there are plenty of fellows to share in the work of keeping CMA running. That's why our Traditions discourage us from taking on too many jobs in a group; no one should ever seem to be the face of the program. If we've been nominated to chair a second or third meeting, we might instead suggest another fellow—someone else who could use the job to help them stay clean. That is itself a kind of service. Or, if we're already sponsoring half a dozen people, we might recommend another fellow who's been eager to do it—that helps two people at once. Ultimately, sharing the wealth serves the fellowship better: The more people who can sponsor, lead meetings, and keep the area running smoothly, the more likely we will all flourish for years to come.

STEP TWELVE

CARRYING THE MESSAGE IN THE WORLD OUTSIDE

What about helping someone who's not in the rooms? Most us will eventually meet a person who's using meth or some other drug and losing control. Or someone we've confided in about our recovery will come to us about a friend in trouble. Shouldn't we share our recovery with people who need help? Yes, of course—but not in the way we might like.

As much as we may want to drag them right away to a CMA meeting, we try to resist the urge. Though it might be obvious to the whole planet that someone is an addict and needs help, until they decide they need that help, our best efforts will probably backfire. In such situations, we remember that CMA is a program of "attraction, not promotion." If we're going about life sober, sane, and happy, well, that is very attractive to someone whose world is falling apart. Being an example—quietly showing that you can do and be anything you want without drugs—is the best way to share our recovery.

In the earliest years of Alcoholics Anonymous, members would actively seek out "prospects." (Mostly salesmen themselves, AA's founders used a lot of sales terminology.) But recovering addicts don't really do this anymore. In the first place, people all over the world know about Twelve Step programs now—they know where we are. And proselytizing almost never works anyway. Everyone has to come to the realization that they need help on their own. As tempting as it is to reach out and save an addict in trouble, it's often counterproductive. Taking someone to a meeting before they have the desire to come themselves may poison the experience for them. A year or two later, when they're truly ready to surrender, they may not trust us.

THE TWELVE STEPS

Sometimes, the person we want to help will be a fellow who's left CMA. Maybe they were put off by the program's spirituality, or had an uncomfortable interaction with someone in the rooms, or simply decided they missed having wine at dinner. Whatever the reason, it's best to let them figure out for themselves if they want to return. Our own painful memories of trying to go it alone keep us active in recovery; but it took some of us a long time to come in or to come back after a relapse. We find it best to let a wandering friend know we're available if they ever want to talk, but to otherwise let them take their own journey. They'll return when they're ready, if they want to. And if they never come back—some people don't get sober, and some find other ways to get their life together—there's no reason for us to feel threatened. We stick with the Steps because they work for us.

We may want to dive in and rescue someone who's struggling to tread water, but it rarely works. And it's not good for the rescuer, either. We can never be more emotionally invested in someone's recovery than they are. We risk putting ourselves in precarious or triggering situations. (For this reason, if someone in a gray area calls us to help get rid of drugs or paraphernalia, for example, we ask a fellow to come along. Making such "Twelve Step calls" on our own is too dangerous.) Ultimately, we don't want to end up in a codependent situation, enabling someone to keep using by shielding them from the consequences of addiction. Of course we want to help anyone who's in physical danger. But as painful as it might be to watch someone hitting bottom, that may be the one thing that finally inspires them to get help.

It's best to "be the change we wish to see in the world," as a wise man once said. We live our life in recovery with integrity and purpose, but we don't preach about it. If someone is curious about CMA, we tell them what works for us.

When they want to go to a meeting, we offer to come along. And when they're ready to open up about their experience, we listen. We share about our own journey with crystal and other drugs when it relates to theirs, and we say a bit about how the fellowship helps us stay sober. Listening is the main thing, however: An addict needs to feel like they can relate to people who've stopped using. But more important, they need to feel heard.

Recovery has become our home, and we'd like nothing better than to share it with other addicts in need of a solution. But all we can do is hold the door open. Whether they walk through it or not is up to them.

ALL OF OUR AFFAIRS

During our first year of sobriety, the fellowship offered us a safe haven—and it always will. But eventually, we began to feel comfortable again out in the real world, mingling with "civilians." We're able to practice the principles of the program in all our affairs because, well, we have other affairs! Friendships and family, careers and vocations, all sorts of pastimes, silly or serious—we can return to all of it. The Steps have been described as a "bridge back to life," and we've crossed over it. Service in CMA is a great way to ensure we don't leave the program behind. Because while we don't want to ever be stuck on the bridge, avoiding life's challenges, neither do we want to leave it in the past, forgetting what we've been through and what we owe the fellowship.

You've heard about anonymity in the rooms, the idea that "what we hear here, stays here." It's not just a matter of protecting each other's privacy and the reputation of the program—anonymity keeps us humble, and that attitude is indispensable if we're to stay sober. But the transformation we experience in recovery definitely travels with us into the rest of our lives. Many of us only figured out how to interact with people again in CMA. It gave us a safe place to make mistakes and learn from them. What happens in the rooms is more and more likely to happen outside of them, too: What we *do* here, we do everywhere.

We probably realized this when our fellows introduced us to the concept of surrender, in Step Three. Accepting people as they are—whether they're our partners, children, bosses, rivals, friends, or whoever—can be hard. But the benefits are obvious. The Serenity Prayer was like a life vest in the early days, when we were drowning in uncomfortable feelings and cravings could strike without warning. We began to reach for it at other moments, too. We couldn't handle any situation in our using days. Practicing acceptance, now we can.

The inventory and amends process has become second nature. We're quick to see our part in conflicts; we know when we're operating out of fear, and we're tuned in to our character defects. When we screw up, apologizing and making things right is no longer unthinkable. Our experience has shown us our humanity. In addiction, we almost lost our lives, and we definitely lost touch with our spirits. In recovery, we put away our pride and set aside our expectations. In short, today we live our whole lives guided by the Steps. We aim for progress; when we stumble, we get back up.

In the fellowship, we grow more and more willing to serve others, and we bring this spirit to the rest of our lives as well. We show up for our families, becoming better partners, parents, and children. We show up at work, readily joining the team and giving our best effort. And we show up for our communities, taking great pleasure in volunteer work, activism, the arts, and other pursuits. We look for ways to give back wherever we go. Charity begins at home, they say, and now we are at home in the world.

STEP TWELVE

CONNECTION AND FREEDOM

At the beginning of this book, we said the Steps could set you on a spiritual path, if you were willing. But we made only one promise: Working the Steps, you can stay sober. Your journey in recovery will not likely follow a straight line. It's up to each of us to learn from whatever twists and turns we encounter. Our fellows always urge us to take lessons as they're offered. If we do so, we have no doubt about it. We never have to use again.

But the life we promise, free from active addiction, is only the beginning. Abstinence gives us a blank canvas; recovery offers us paints and brushes. It's up to us to pick them up and make our life a work of art.

One word you won't find anywhere in the Steps is "connection"—yet it's at the heart of everything we do. In addiction we were isolated from other people and our own spirits. We sought to cut ourselves off from the universe, and going it alone nearly took our lives. At each stage of the journey, we've drawn closer to our fellow human beings. This last Step tells us to make a habit of it. We could summarize Twelve thus: "Now that you've reconnected to the world, go out and share that good feeling." Recovery has shown us many paradoxes, but this is probably the most beautiful one: With each connection we make, we become more and more free.

We never put our recovery behind us. We have calmed our mental obsession, but our treatment requires us to remain vigilant one day at a time. As long as we have the desire to stop using, we'll keep working the Steps. With the perspective of longer sobriety and greater emotional growth, we can learn new truths about ourselves and the world each time we revisit this work. And we draw even deeper insights when we share the Steps with others.

We who are recovering in Crystal Meth Anonymous are eager to share our program with you, if you want it.

THE TWELVE STEPS

Following this simple program of suggested Steps, we have opened the door to a new life.

Yesterday we were paralyzed—
today we're changing moment by moment.
Yesterday we hated ourselves—
today we like who we're becoming.
Yesterday we were isolated—
today we treasure connections old and new.
Yesterday we said no to everything—
today we say yes.
Yesterday we shut out the world—
today we dance to the rhythm of the universe.
Yesterday we were trapped—
today we are free.